LEADING ADULT LEARNERS

Handbook for All Christian Groups

DELIA HALVERSON

Abingdon Press
Nashville

LEADING ADULT LEARNERS: HANDBOOK FOR ALL CHRISTIAN GROUPS

Copyright © 1995 by Abingdon Press

This book is printed on recycled, acid-free paper.

Library of Congress Cataloging-in-Publication Data

Halverson, Delia Touchton.
    Leading adult learners: handbook for all Christian groups/Delia Halverson.
        p.   cm.
    Includes bibliographical references.
    ISBN 0-687-00223-0 (pbk.: alk. paper)
    1. Christian education of adults. 2. Sunday schools. 3. Church group work. I. Title.
BV1550.H32   1995
268'.434—dc20   95-16970
                                                                                   CIP

95 96 97 98 99 00 01 02 03 04 05 — 10 9 8 7 6 5 4 3 2 1

MANUFACTURED IN THE UNITED STATES OF AMERICA

*To
the many Christian educators,
professional and volunteer,
with whom I share this ministry.
A special appreciation
to
the members of
Christian Educator's Fellowship,
who give me backbone and support.*

CONTENTS

FOREWORD

People spend most of their lives as adults. From the age of twenty years or so to the age of eighty years or so, we are adults—sixty years! What a long time—yet it goes so quickly! We constantly wonder where the days, months, years, and decades have gone.

Like children and youth, adults change, grow, and learn all of our lives. Much of our time is spent in groups, some quite small groups such as families and close friends, and some much larger such as at our places of work, or at the church. Hundreds of thousands of adults attend adult classes every week in churches—some large, some small. This handbook is for persons in those classes. It is not so much a book to read, as a book to use. The interested adult needs to selectively look for those particular things that seem important. Here are many resources, ideas, and suggestions concerning

- who we are as adults and why we are attracted to groups
- how to organize, sustain, and invigorate adult classes
- how to teach, lead, and stimulate adults to think, feel, serve, and pray.

Start where you feel a need and move on to other sections later.

My wife and I, in our early 70s, attend a class in which the average age is 78 to 80 years, and several members are in their 90s. The class is about fifty years old, and is going strong—even though canes are used by many members. New members join our class regularly—we learn from both our lessons and from one another, we have occasional social events, we give liberally to our own benevolent fund, and we care for each other carefully. There are good ideas in this book for our class.

Delia Halverson has assembled and assessed many of the best resources written about adult learning and adult church groups in recent years. I found three of the most helpful sections for me concern

- faith development
- prayer
- service learning

You will find others that interest you, but a few comments about these three are as follows:

Adults and Faith

In the last three decades a great deal has been written about how faith develops and changes during one's life span. The author summarizes much of that thought and research.

What has happened to your faith in the past thirty years? I have changed during the period between my fortieth and seventieth years. I have grown a beard, and it has become pure white. During this time I have changed directions in my career, and now I have retired. My body has become quite limited in its functions, and my faith has been tried and changed. Like many other adults I have reached out to others in my various groups, as I have been forced to reexamine and modify my faith. My adult class has played an important role in my faith development.

Prayer

Delia Halverson emphasizes the importance of adults studying, practicing, and growing in prayer. This is an important emphasis, as adults in groups and alone look at their spiritual growth. Many readers will find fine suggestions concerning improvement in the prayer practice of their class.

Service Learning

We know that in the very act of service we are often motivated to learn. This book lists a variety of creative service projects which you may find helpful. Service projects both unify and motivate adult groups and classes.

Adults want and need to grow, and many find adult classes vital in that process. I teach large and small, young and older adult classes each year. I am continually impressed by their enthusiasm and interest. They want to be better parents and grandparents. They want to deepen their personal spiritual lives. They want to improve their relationships with others, and with God. Nearly without exception they believe their class helps them. Many will find ideas and good suggestions in this handbook.

Dick Murray
Dallas, Texas

INTRODUCTION

After an earnest plea for *just anyone* to take the leadership of the class, the outgoing president suggested that they divide the year up into quarters so that no one had an overwhelming job. The leadership did not require teaching, only seeing that the teaching slots were filled. Finally, class members began to volunteer to take on a quarter at a time. With fear and trembling two women offered to take a quarter's leadership six months in the future.

This was a real step in faith for one of the women, because she had never held such a leadership position before. How do you take over leadership of a class with no previous experience? Where do you begin? Just what does it entail? Where do you go for help?

For two years I have led a program of self-directed studies during the summer for lay and clergy leaders in the church. The most popular study was on organizing and resourcing adult classes. As I prepared the curriculum for the study I realized that there was no comprehensive book that combined materials for all leadership in adult classes. I found books on characteristics of various stages of adulthood, stages of faith, and how to teach adults. Curriculum materials gave excellent helps for teaching specific topics. I searched through several magazines for articles about organization of classes, special projects, social events, and publicity. Finally, equipped with an armload of magazines and curricula and a box of books, I developed an outline suggesting sections of books and various articles for study.

Even with over thirty years of experience in Christian education I found it difficult to bring together materials. Yet we expect persons to hold a class together with no knowledge of where to go for help. I began to see why my friend who had no experience in leadership was overwhelmed when she volunteered to lead her class for a quarter.

Out of this enlightenment the idea for this book came into form. As I traveled about the country consulting and teaching workshops, the idea met with approval. And so now you have it all under one cover: information for all adult class leadership gathered in one place.

I've also included forms and charts that I find helpful as I work with adults. I hope that they will be time-savers for you.

Why is this book important? Because adult classes are of prime importance if we are to spread Christ's gospel and share the Good News with other adults. The "future" may be with the children and youth, but the future is built on the present, and the present lies in our adults today.

The church of the future must work toward a central mission. Taking Paul's suggestion of being all one body, we might symbolically consider:

- *education* as the head of the body, studying the scriptures and ways to carry out our faith in the world and empowering the whole body to function as one.

- *stewardship* as the heart of the body, receiving God's gifts and responding to those gifts.
- *worship* as the hands of the body, lifted in continual praise to God.
- *evangelism* as the arms of the body, reaching out to others in love.
- *mission* as the feet of the body, taking us to places we can be of service to others, sharing God with the world.
- *the administrative positions* (such as finance, communications, staff/parish, etc.) as the vital organs of the body, breathing breath and life into the whole body of Christ.

It takes all parts of the body to function at our full potential and to remain healthy. We must work together for the wholeness of our ministry.

CHAPTER 1

Educating Adults— More Than Book Learning

Classes for adults just aren't what they used to be, and rightfully so. Adults aren't what they used to be! Life circumstances change, interests change, needs change. Each church must adapt adult education to its own situation.

Some small churches may find adult education appropriate in varying situations without a need for ongoing classes, where large or mega-churches will find a need for ongoing classes as well as short term learning experiences. Learning happens inside and outside the classroom. Developing a class unit simply gives a caring atmosphere for learning. This is particularly important in large churches, where it is impossible for the whole congregation to talk together, sharing problems and concerns outside the building after the Sunday service.

Our family's first experience with actually belonging to a mega-church surprised us. We had worshiped in large churches, but we had never actually belonged to a church with more than 350 members. In fact, prior to their high school years, our children had never even lived in a town with as many residents as our new church had members! We expected anonymity. Surely, we thought, with so many people we'd never find a church family. Were we surprised! We discovered the most friendly church we'd ever experienced.

As we worked in the church we began to identify two primary elements that brought this about. First, the staff made a concerted effort of caring which spread to the whole congregation. The other element that made this church unique was the *strength of the adult Sunday school classes* and other ongoing adult groups. These acted as mini-congregations within the larger congregation. Within these small vital units, adults and their families found love and caring in depth. And through the ministry of the classes, they reached out in concerned love to others. These classes were not just book learning. Here we found real life learning.

Adult education makes up the real world of our developing civilization.

- Every time we wrestle with how to relate to another person, there is education.
- Every time we wonder about God's relationship with the world, there is education.
- Every time we adjust an idea that doesn't work, there is education.

It may not be organized. There may not be a teacher standing before us, telling us what to do. In fact, the learning process probably works best when we try adjusting it ourselves instead of being told how to go about it.

Since people first began to wonder about the greater force that made this world, controls it, and keeps it in action, adults have been involved in religious education. The Bible itself charts our developing concepts and understandings of God and of how God relates to us.

And so adult Christian education involves all of life: how we understand God; how we relate to God; how we relate to other people; and living all of this out in our daily lives. And, yes, we learn about this from the book we call the Bible, but we also learn about it from life and from those around us. Adult Christian education is more than book learning!

In mainline denominations, today's adults are reported to be most interested in studying, learning more about, or being involved in these ten areas:

- The Bible   77%
- Developing a personal relationship with Jesus   75%
- Improving skills at showing love and concern   74%
- Learning how to be a good spouse or parent   74%
- Applying my faith to daily living   73%
- Making more friends at church   69%
- Learning how Christians make moral decisions   68%
- Getting help with my spiritual journey   62%
- Having greater sense of community at church   62%
- Helping members who are experiencing hardship   59%[1]

Why in the church?

A church cannot function well without good adult education.

1) *Adults must learn in order to teach children.* (A 1988 study indicates that at no time in a child's or youth's life is any peer influence greater than that of his or her parents'.[2])

2) *Adults shape the future only when they set future plans in relation to past human experiences.*

3) *Adults are the leaders of the church, directing its ministry and making decisions.*

But why should we have Sunday school classes for adults at all? Why not simply "graduate" from Sunday school like we do from high school and forget about education?

Adults and education

In reality, most adults today don't forget about education. They simply don't recognize that they encounter learning experiences every day. Adults continue to learn after they leave high school, throughout their middle years, and after they retire from an active career, even if they ignore formal teaching and education.

Children think that adults know all that there is to know. Just sit beside a three-year-old and try to answer the many questions!

On the other hand, a youth seems to wonder how adults (especially one's parents) can live for so many years and not have learned *anything!*

As adults, however, we realize that neither the child nor the youth fully understands the learning struggles of adulthood. Just when we think we have life in control, life comes along and knocks us for a loop, and we must once again learn something new.

Learning is an ongoing event. The nationwide trend for adult learning continues to grow, as evidenced in community courses, continuing education requirements by employers, and the vast publication of self-help books. Even if our numbers are declining in church education, we cannot simply hang our heads and claim that adults don't want to learn. Instead we must analyze our learning opportunity methods. In other words, let's look at the system.

Adult learning and adult teaching may not be one and the same. Adult learning is more than reading a lesson, listening to a teacher, and perhaps answering some questions. Adult learning happens throughout each day. Consequently, adult learning goes on in every part of your adult Sunday school class program. For that reason, all leaders of adult classes share responsibility for setting the stage for adult learning, whether functioning as a social chairpersons or teachers.

Adults learn through personal reflection

Personal reflection occurs in many different settings. Actually, it's so common that we often fail to recognize it. Each time you look at a stranger on the street or in a store and wonder about the person's life circumstances, you practice a personal reflection. In adult classes we use something similar called role play. Students confront a specific life situation and act out or verbalize how they would react under those circumstances.

When we read a newspaper or listen to a lecture, although we may not make a verbal comment, we bounce the ideas around in our minds and decide whether we agree with the other person's viewpoint. If we don't agree, then we ponder why.

Personal reflection happens in adult classes every Sunday. Your class may want to offer some additional opportunities for this type of learning such as retreats and other formats suggested in chapter 9.

Adults learn through relationships and informal discussion

Ongoing classes need to spend as much effort in developing relationships and providing informal discussion time as in developing lesson plans. By joining an ongoing class, adults indicate their need for relationships. Small discussion classes, or large classes that routinely divide into small discussion groups, can develop relationships as they study. However, the large class that does not divide into smaller groups needs informal visiting time before or after the formal study time to bring this about. A coffee or fellowship time often provides this.

Trips and social events may also build relationships. In these situations adults learn from one another and from their experiences, whether they realize it or not. Look at the project ideas and social event suggestions in chapter 9 and consider some of these for your class.

Adults learn through the arts

The arts offer learning experiences for both the observer and the participant. Too often we ignore drama, poetry, music, and graphic arts when we think about adult education. Recognize various art expressions as learning opportunities. Turn to chapter 6 for ideas for such learning activities.

Adults learn through hands-on projects

Here is the opportunity for your class to work with other areas in the church. Jesus did not simply tell his story of the Good Samaritan as a good story, but he followed it with the instruction, "Go and do likewise." He knew that no learning is complete until we actually put it into practice. We must recognize hands-on projects as learning experiences as well as outreach missions of the church. Discuss such projects with your church committee on missions or look at chapter 9 of this book for possible projects.

Bible-centered and life-centered study

Adults of different ages learn differently, and various adults in all age groupings also learn differently. Adult learning should be even more personalized than that of children, yet we often try to lump all adults together and say, "This is what every adult should study."

Both Bible and life-centered studies in the church should be biblically based. The primary difference is the approach. Bible-centered classes study specific sections of the Bible and apply life circumstances to the scripture. Life-centered classes study life events and situations and apply scripture teachings to those.

A good many years ago as I was debating whether to take some theological courses, a Christian education professor told me, "I should think that anyone really interested in Christian education would take every opportunity possible just to study."

I'm sorry that I didn't feel comfortable enough at the time to stand up for my convictions about adult education. In fact, I'm not sure I knew then just what my convictions were. I did know that although in the past I had enjoyed learning for the joy of learning, at the time I spoke to the professor, I felt that I was more pressed to learn ways to solve some of my problems than to study for the joy of studying. If the learning had no direct bearing on my needs, I only became frustrated with the time spent on the endeavor.

I've worked with many adults in their study programs since then, and I've heard their reasons for joining a Sunday school class or study group. With our busy schedules today, adults have an even greater need than they did twenty years ago to concentrate on specific learning that helps them deal with their daily problems. The challenge is to find a center of focus for learning and then to allow that to broaden as we study. Although we will never solve all of our problems, if we feel that we have a place to turn with our problems, *then* new avenues open to us and excite us with new challenges. If we feel that we have help with our life situations, *then* we can enjoy the luxury of satisfying our desire for learning.

Every church, no matter the size, should offer both Bible-centered and life-centered study for adults, whether the variety of study takes place in the same class or in separate classes. A growing church needs to continually develop classes of both types.

A 1988 national study of Protestant congregations stated that an educational process which nurtures growth in mature faith:

- emphasizes building an understanding of faith applied to political and social issues and an understanding of oppression and injustice.
- emphasizes life experiences as occasions for spiritual insight.
- creates a sense of community in which people help each other develop faith and values.
- emphasizes the natural unfolding of faith and recognizes each person's faith journey as unique.
- strongly encourages independent thinking and questioning.

In addition, educational content should also emphasize:

- biblical knowledge and understanding.
- multicultural awareness.
- global awareness and understanding.
- moral decision making.[3]

CHAPTER 2

Exploring Faith Development

I find it helpful to separate faith from beliefs in my mind. Faith may be defined as our relationship with God. The Hebrew word *emunah,* may be translated as a total trust and confidence in God.

My beliefs are what I believe at any given point. As a child, my literal mind conjured up a very literal God who made it rain by poking holes in the clouds with an ice pick and then pouring water over the holes. Needless to say, I no longer hold to that belief. Much of what I believed as a child has changed and continues to change as I study and grow closer to God.

We expect our faith (our relationship with God) to deepen and grow throughout our lives. Faith development does not automatically come with years, but rather with experience in our relationship with God. Consequently, you will find adults in the same class at different stages of faith.

The mission of the church is to assist one another in development of faith, and we do this through worshiping and studying together.

In recent years many theologians have studied the development of our faith. Although they assigned different labels to the process, these theologians all agree that we experience faith long before we put labels on what we experience. They also agree that our association with other people plays an important role in our faith development, and that at some point it is very natural to spend time inquiring about or questioning our faith beliefs. Central to all of their theories on the maturity of our faith is our relationship to other people, sharing God's love.

Stages of faith

The book *Stages of Faith* by James Fowler suggests that our first experiences of faith begin with birth.[1] The early years of childhood are a pre-stage of undifferentiated faith. By the constancy of those around us who are providers, we initially experience loyalty and dependability, two foundations for our concept of God. The transition to stage one of faith begins as a child learns language and develops thought and use of symbols in speech and ritual play.

The first stage of faith development is identifed as *Intuitive Projective Faith*. The child learns and develops by imitating. During this stage the child is greatly influenced by examples, moods, actions, and stories. It is a time of rapid imaginative development, occurring before the child can yet distinguish clearly between imagination and reality. Because of the patchwork nature of knowledge at this stage, children fill in the gaps with fantasy. Most of us move through this stage between the ages of three to seven.

The second stage of faith is called *Mythic: Literal*. It is typical of elementary-age children. During this stage the community of faith supplies stories. The beliefs and symbols of our religion become personal and can take on a literal meaning. When we begin to realize and acknowledge that there are different stories, we are naturally pushed into stage three, a time of pulling the stories together and forming a conventional faith that we can believe.

The *Synthetic-Conventional Faith* of stage three typically happens during adolescence, when there is an upheaval in physical and emotional development. The adolescent works to pull the varying parts of his or her world together: the community, the school, the church, the family, and his or her peers. The person at this stage begins to form an identity, but the teen is not yet sure enough of this identity to step outside of himself or herself and look at it from an objective point of view.

Stage four, the *Individuative-Reflective Faith,* begins when the person is ready to take responsibility for his or her own commitment and beliefs, looking at symbols with the question "What do they mean?" and asking of heretofore conventional beliefs the question "Is this what I really believe?" In this stage we look for logical and clear distinctions between varying beliefs, looking at them all and making decisions. The usual time for this stage is during the early to mid-twenties, but it can begin earlier.

In the *Conjunctive* stage five we begin to pull these decisions together into a faith that we can truly acknowledge as our own, and we are no longer threatened by others' beliefs. In stage five we see faith as unifying; we are part of the faith but are still looking at it, examining it.

Stage six is labeled *Universalizing Faith*. Only a few in our world ever reach this stage. Those few have become totally immersed in the being of God and yet see the universal life as a whole.[2]

Styles of faith

The book *Will Our Children Have Faith* by John Westerhoff suggests four styles of faith development. As we move through these styles, we do not leave one behind for another, but rather add additional styles as we go along, as a tree adds rings of growth with each year. Each style is important for a mature faith.

In the first, an *experienced faith,* we experience much of the personality of God through other people. By experiencing the love of a parent, the infant begins to form his or her attitude toward God. Experiential learning (drama, arts, creative movement, role play) contributes to this in the classroom of children, youth, and adults. Congregational worship also offers nourishment in our experiential faith style.

The *affiliated faith* begins when a child learns to relate to his or her peers. The fellowship of an adult class feeds this faith style. God made us in community or in relationship with other persons, and through this fellowship we draw close to God.

The *searching faith* usually begins in the late teens or early twenties. On occasion it begins earlier or later, and some adults never feel comfortable searching and inquiring into their beliefs. We consider the faith stories we have been told and review them again and again, making our own decisions about just what we believe.

The *owned faith* comes about as we develop a personal belief of which we are certain. We have searched our beliefs and acknowledge them as our own. Other persons' professions of different beliefs don't threaten us. The beliefs we hold have integrity and demand action. However, we do not stop inquiring here. For inquiry is important all through our lives in order to maintain a healthy faith.

Vertical/horizontal faith

A person with a mature faith focuses on a relationship with God (vertical dimension) and with others (horizontal dimension).

- Integrated faith—representing a high level of faith maturity, focusing on both God and service to others.
- Vertical faith—representing a life-transforming relationship with God, but not consistent in devotion to serving others.
- Horizontal faith—representing consistent devotion to serving others, but without a life-transforming relationship to God.
- Undeveloped faith—representing neither devotion to serving others nor a life-transforming relationship to God.[3] This theory uses Matthew 22:34-39.

A study of effective Christian education by Search Institute found eight core dimensions of faith. The person with faith maturity:

- trusts in God's saving grace and believes firmly in the humanity and divinity of Jesus;
- experiences a sense of personal well-being, security, and peace;
- integrates faith and life, seeing work, family, social relationships, and political choices as part of one's religious life;
- seeks spiritual growth through study, reflection, prayer, and discussion with others;
- seeks to be part of a community of believers in which people give witness to their faith and support and nourish one another;
- holds life-affirming values, including commitment to racial and gender equality, affirmation of cultural and religious diversity, and a personal sense of responsibility for the welfare of others;
- advocates social and global change to bring about greater social justice; and
- serves humanity, consistently and passionately, through acts of love and justice.[4]

Faith advocates and clarifiers

Both advocates and clarifiers are important for adults. Advocates tell the story, point the way, and offer examples. Clarifiers stand on neutral ground, lift up dilemmas, provoke thought, and encourage inquiry. Ideally an adult teacher works in both arenas.

I had a theology professor once who told me that unless my belief could stand up under questioning, then I'd better find another belief. He gave us permission to question any beliefs we held. This didn't mean that he never shared his beliefs with us. In fact, had he refused to share his beliefs we would have been hesitant of sharing ours. But when he shared, it was in a co-learning atmosphere. We understood just where he stood during our conversations, but he never forced his belief down our throats and always listened attentively to our inquiring minds.

Jesus modeled the clarifier role when he lifted up the dilemma of healing on the Sabbath and encouraged his listeners to inquire into their beliefs (Luke 6:6-11). He also made his listeners probe their thoughts in Matthew 21:23-27 when they asked by whose authority he spoke.

CHAPTER 3

Characterizing
Adult Sunday School Classes

Adult Sunday school classes come in all sizes and formats. Generally, the size of the class and the identity of its members help to determine the format.

Currently I belong to a class with members who range in age from their early thirties to mid eighties. The discussion format and life-centered subject matter draw members of every age grouping. Such age difference is a rare occurrence in most churches, but we enjoy a delightful gathering of personalities. Maxine, who just celebrated her seventy-ninth birthday, says that she joined the class because it helps her to stay young. Most of the younger members joined the class when it was first formed as a young adult class.

Identifying adults

Quite normally, adult classes in most churches tend to develop around persons in specific age groupings or persons whose children are at certain stages of growth.

Young Adults are generally considered to be persons of post high school age and those in their twenties. A better identification might be persons who are dealing with new choices in career, marriage, community location, first apartments or homes, children, community or church responsibilities, and faith beliefs. (See information on Generation X at the end of this chapter.)

Middle Adults range through their thirties and forties. However, many persons in their early thirties consider themselves young adults and still deal with some young adult issues, and a growing number of persons in their early fifties consider themselves middle adults. Most of these adults have children and the usual frustrations and joys accompanying raising a family. Generally, the middle adults are also reconciling themselves to the reality that they may never attain some of the high goals that they set for themselves in their youth. This can cause depression and crisis in relationships. All of these situations can create a common tie within a caring class. (See information on Baby Boomers at the end of this chapter.)

New Seniors (or Active Seniors) generally are in their fifties and sixties, although some persons in their seventies can certainly fall into this category. At this point the children are leaving home or have recently left home, creating a pull between a new independence and loneliness on the part of the parents. As many of these children return home to live (boomerang), the parent/child relationship must change to adult/adult relationships. Some of these class members become grandparents, and some deal with the fact that they may never be grandparents if their children choose to remain childless. Other class members may find themselves parenting their grandchildren. They may also find themselves in a parenting role for their own parents. This group continues to have an active lifestyle and seek goal-directed activities. They expect to spend their time meaningfully in the church, or they will find another outlet for their energy. Instead of recalling yesterday, they talk and plan for tomorrow, anticipating retirement as a time to work and study and serve, as well as a time to play. (See information on the Silent Generation at the end of this chapter.)

Older Adults deal with the slowing down of their own bodies and those of their spouses and friends. Many of them are still mentally alert but begin to question their worth in society. They need opportunities to enhance their self-esteem. They need to look at their past contributions to life with pride and to continue to find ways to be in service. (See information on the GI Generation at the end of this chapter.)

Your class members make up the underlying structure of your class. It is important to know the members and to recognize how they mold the class. The "Adult Class Information Survey" in the appendix will help, but nothing takes the place of face to face conversations. As you talk about vacations you learn whether a person likes to be in large crowds or seeks out places of solitude. As you discuss the problems of parenthood you recognize whether they give priority to acquiring material possessions or to relationships with their children. Discussion of recent movies or television shows often indicates values. Develop opportunities to spend time in conversation.

Take inventory of your class, listing each name and some information about that person, using such questions as:

? What sort of background? (rural/city/small town/inner city)

? Marital status? (never married/intentionally single/expects to marry some day/courting/married ___ years/formerly married/married again)

? Family? (ages of children/extended family in home/blended family)

? Educational level? (high school graduate/left high school without graduating/GED graduate/college student/higher education degree)

? Employment? (unemployed/new on job/part-time employment/settled in job/expecting retirement/retired)

? Member of church? (full member/affiliate or associate member/visitor/active non-member)

? Physical status? (prime of health/disability/allergies/health problems)

? Travel or military experience? (places visited/veteran)

After the formation of an adult class, the class matures as the charter members mature. The "Life Cycle of a Class" at the end of this chapter will help you to understand the status of your class.

The book *Five Audiences—Identifying Groups in Your Church* outlines five categories of adults. You will find these helpful as you consider study plans and activities for your class.

- *Fellowship*—enjoy use of media, seek stability in teachers, enjoy informal discussion, high value on relationships, no strong institutional ties, desire curriculum relevant to them today
- *Traditionalists*—Bible oriented, beliefs important, usually enjoy dated curriculum and regular teacher(s), prefer lectures, loyal to church and/or Sunday school class, enjoy traditional classroom patterns and resist changes. (*Neo-traditionalists* who recently returned to the faith share theological views with Traditionalists, enjoy Bible or spiritual formation curriculum, look for biblical and theological mentors, are highly influenced by books and magazines, and often switch from one church to another searching for a class or study to meet their needs.)
- *Study*—supervisory and professional careers, tolerant to positions other than their own, study Christian faith/life application, highly ecumenical, prefer to choose their teacher who is co-learner, like good teaching aids, enjoy curriculum relevant to today, relate well to others
- *Social Action Group*—people-centered and service-oriented careers, faith is private matter and place more importance on social action than spiritual disciplines, view church/class as launching pad for action and want the teacher to help explore needs the class might meet, little patience with those who do not share their concerns
- *Multiple Interest Group*—see views halfway between other groups; usually combining fellowship with another area, majority of congregation, respect others' views, comfortable with wide variety of teaching methods and curricula.[1]

Adult education emphasis in churches

According to the three year study of 561 congregations in five mainline denominations (representing 85% of "mainline Protestantism") the following emphases are placed on adult education:

- learning how to apply faith to everyday life   75%
- developing Bible knowledge   74%
- providing fellowship and social interaction   71%
- theological reflection on human experience   61%[2]

Formats for classes

Each adult class develops its usual format, but since adults learn in many different ways, offering several study styles during the year affords an opportunity for greater learning.

➡ *Discussion classes* work best when the leader functions as a facilitator. The leader may give a brief presentation or the class members may have read some information before class, then the leader encourages persons to reflect on the idea or subject. If the class is larger than ten or twelve, it is best that members divide into groups of four to six for the discussion so that everyone has an opportunity to speak. Sometimes the small groups may discuss different aspects of the subject and report back to the larger group. If the larger class does not break down into small groups for discussion, then the discussion is often dominated by certain class members who feel comfortable to speak up in a large group.

➡ *Lecture classes (or informal presentations)* are probably the most common in churches. When well done, a lecture offers information and insights and encourages reflection on the subject. Persons may agree or disagree with the speaker without having to argue a point. Many times lectures are followed by brief discussion periods. Here again, if the class is large, the members should be divided into smaller groups or asked to discuss their thoughts with one or two persons sitting near them. To help the learning experience for lecture classes, encourage note taking. The notes should be a method of encouraging additional thinking on the subject after the session.

➡ *Mini-worship services* are sometimes popular in larger classes. The class sings several hymns, makes announcements, has a short devotion, takes an offering, and the teacher speaks. Such classes need additional time for class members to interact, perhaps around a coffee pot or at frequent socials.

➡ *Self-directed study* may offer additional learning for members of ongoing classes or may be independent of classes. See the appendix for a form you might use to develop your own self-directed studies.

➡ *Homebound* class members need to be included in every way possible. Make tapes of your class presentations to share with those homebound. Appoint someone as liaison to keep them informed. If your church has several homebound persons, consider a telephone hookup between them each Sunday morning with a Sunday school teacher on the line at the church. Several churches have developed successful homebound classes. Contact your local telephone company for help in implementing such a program.

Short-term studies

Consider offering both ongoing classes and short-term studies for adults. The short-term studies may range from a one-time speaker to a multi-course offering. You may plan short-term studies during your regular Sunday school hour or sponsor such studies at other times.

● Sunday morning has become the norm for adult classes in most churches. It is convenient because children also attend classes. In advertising short-term studies on Sunday morning, be sure to encourage any regular ongoing class members who elect to take a course to move back into their classes after they complete the specific study.

- Sometimes a three-hour period early on Saturday morning works well for parents. (Always offer child care or learning activities for children.)
- Retired adults may enjoy a weekday study including a noon meal.
- Employed persons may find it convenient to meet at a restaurant en route to work or during the lunch hour. (Keep such meetings brief, recognizing their schedules.)
- Short studies for committee members, choir members, ushers, acolytes, etc. that relate to the spiritual understanding of their responsibilities. These may take place at the beginning of their regular meetings.

Smorgasbord of study

If your class is large, you might try a smorgasbord of study, or you might want to combine with other classes for such a study. Several subjects are selected and leaders are assigned. Everyone meets for fellowship at the beginning of the class, and then moves to a selected area to study a particular subject for that day. The class(es) may be divided into groups and rotated each week to a different subject, or students may sign up ahead for specific studies on specific days.

Table Talk

A church in Iowa tried a different type of class for the summer months. They titled the class "Table Talk," using the models of Martin Luther, who often discussed theological matters at dinner with his seminary students, and Karl Barth, who told his students that every pastor should read the Bible and a good newspaper. Each Sunday the class (adults and some high schoolers) met over coffee, tea, pastries, and the morning newspaper. They selected given articles from the paper and discussed them from a biblical perspective. With such a class, different members may lead the discussion, but you will need to have one person consciously attentive to ways to parallel the discussion to a story or teaching from the Bible.

Consider using the same format to dig further into the sermon topic of the morning. It is important that persons hear the sermon before the class period.

Generation X

Profile	• born during the sixties, seventies and eighties • also called the Thirteenth Generation (thirteenth generation of American citizens), Baby Busters (numbers of births down) and the Lost or Gap Generation • born of parents who looked out for number one and had no firm religious convictions • parents exercised an option to have children, two-income families, changing sex roles, limited resources, violent models, mobile lifestyles, declining job markets • some from homes of plenty, but many from homes below poverty level • a generation with median income of $10,000, many without jobs • expected to have greatest impact on money and marketplace
Characteristics	• independent, view themselves as realists and survivors, risk-takers • skeptical of people, let down by national figures they admired • flexible, anxious to cut to the action without wasting time talking • work at jobs to enjoy leisure and expect to have several careers in life • question commitment to marriage and raising children • good at finding alternative ways around impossible situations
What Xers want from Church	• a redefinition of Christian value: life can be abundant without abundance • a willingness to listen and offer understanding, but encouragement to seek their *own* answers and make their *own* decisions • pragmatic Christianity, including ALL of life • involvement of laity in study, worship leadership and decisions • biblical emphasis on survival during hardships • experiential learning with practical applications to any spiritual decisions • opportunity for hands-on mission to persons *before* learning about Christ • action rather than polite conversation about ideologies • multiple worship styles, time frames, support groups, styles and locations for study, service to others, leadership opportunities • images of diversity of God

Baby Boomers

Profile	• born between 1946 and 1964
	• one in three Americans
	• have 3-D lifestyle • Delayed marriage
	                      • Deferred childbearing
	                      • Divorcing couples
	• often dictate change because of their sheer numbers
	• not all swinging and rich: many average $15,000 or less income
	• generally unchurched and biblically illiterate
	• baptized as infants
	• few joined a church
	• questioning, as they enter mid-life

Characteristics	• two-income families • moms pulled between moving up in career and family devotion • dads more involved with children • materialistic models—peer pressure • no dedication to one denomination or church • tight schedules
What Baby Boomers want from Church	• innovative worship • involvement *before* joining • family involvement • consideration of pressed and erratic time schedules (suppers, babysitting, meeting times clustered, etc.) • short-term assignments and studies • options provided • opportunity to develop common bonds, support systems • because of limited time, they want their time to be useful, not just filled • opportunity to help in an area of their interest • evidence that their commitment makes a difference • service that is people, rather than task, oriented • awareness of and help to oppressed; mission support (financial and hands-on) • support of global peace • more than an informational Bible study, they want studies that affect their lives

	Silent Generation	GI Generation
Profile	<ul><li>born 1925–1942</li><li>raised in Depression/war</li><li>born too soon or too late</li><li>early marriage/child bearing</li><li>dilemma over feminism</li><li>personal (not national) passages</li></ul>	<ul><li>born 1901–1924</li><li>horse/buggy to space travel</li><li>two world wars</li><li>one-income families</li><li>strong civic/government pride</li></ul>
Characteristics	<ul><li>arbitrator/mediator</li><li>adaptive but slow decision makers</li><li>directed to others</li><li>assisting roles/public life</li><li>like to deliberate</li><li>gather facts/opinions</li><li>prefer process to outcome</li></ul>	<ul><li>self-sufficient, aggressive</li><li>strong values</li><li>powerful work ethic</li><li>believe in institutions</li><li>strong denominational ties</li><li>resist change</li></ul>
What they want from Church	<ul><li>advocacy opportunities</li><li>time to reflect before decisions</li><li>help with life situations</li><li>discussion opportunities</li><li>praise for leadership</li><li>change with reason</li><li>people-oriented service</li></ul>	<ul><li>belonging in community</li><li>loyalty</li><li>ownership/own space</li><li>strong Bible study</li><li>emphasis on values</li><li>consistent traditions</li><li>attention to detail</li></ul>

Life Cycle of a Class

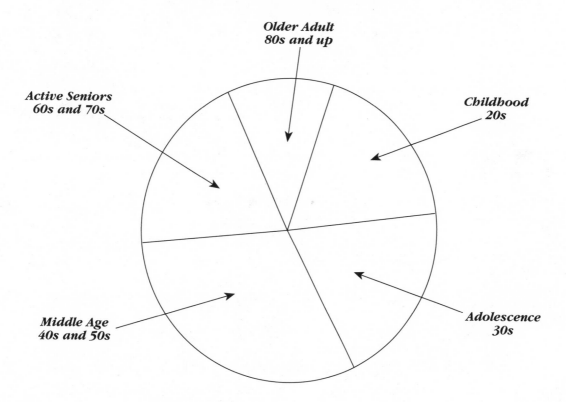

Childhood:
- Look for support in new adult responsibilities.
- Use teachers as role models.
- Inquiring questions in faith.

Adolescence:
- Enjoy family events.
- Look to each other for support in parenting skills.
- Take responsibility for specific projects.
- Move in and out of class as they teach their children's classes but need to maintain contact.
- Typically larger classes will form subgroups for more fellowship and support.

Middle Age:
- Hold key responsibilities in the church.
- Major contributors to church budget.
- Look for mutual support as children move through teen years.
- Need renewed help with spousal relationships or support during divorce.

Active Seniors:
- Social and mission activities often increase with more time and less money. These activities also help to ease the transition of church leadership to younger persons.
- Need support as class members move into retirement and grandparenting.
- Attendance drops as members die, and relationships in class become important after death of a spouse.

Older Adults:
- Physical conditions hamper ability to get out. These conditions and death cause class to experience a sharp attendance drop.
- Morale of class needs boosting, reminding members of contribution they have made as a class to the church.
- Dilemma develops as the room becomes too large for the numbers yet the members want to hold on to the room because it is familiar in an ever changing world.[3]

Forming
New Adult Classes

"**O**ur adult classes are becoming too large."
"We don't seem to be drawing new adults to our Sunday school hour."
"None of the adult classes meet my needs."
"The Young Adult Class has grown too old for new young adults."
"Parents just drop their children off for Sunday school and go down the street to coffee."
"Sunday morning is not a good time for me to attend an adult class."

Churches consider starting new adult classes for many reasons. And all too often such a proposal meets the standard reply:
"BUT I'M AFRAID IT WILL FALL FLAT AND NO ONE WILL COME!"

One couple in a church in Nashville wanted a young adult class and was determined to make it succeed. They went one-on-one among friends, pounded on doors in their apartment house, and told everyone that they *had* to come. The first Sunday ten people attended, and the class continually grew from there.

A few adults in a small-town church in north Georgia wanted a class that offered discussion instead of lecture. They canvassed their friends, found someone to lead the class for the first few weeks, and stepped out with faith and excitement! Within a year the class was larger than either of the other adult classes, and they had a core of teachers among themselves.

One growing adult class found themselves too large for their room. There were no larger rooms, but a smaller one was available. They divided the class, but continued to function as one class by meeting together for coffee at the first of the hour, then going into the two different rooms for their study. Subjects for study were planned in advance, with each room offering a different topic. Individuals chose their room according to their interest in the subjects. As their numbers continued to grow, the class naturally divided itself and eventually became two separate classes. The classes still enjoy one or two social events together each year. Occasionally they choose to study together during the summer when many of the class members are out of town.

Church growth authorities tell us that in order to stay on the growing edge, a congregation should begin at least one new Sunday school class a year. Often that class will be of adult age.

The function of an adult class includes social and group building time as well as time for spiritual development. An adult class should offer a supportive atmosphere where each person may grow as a Christian. Adult classes become mini-congregations and may fill social needs as well as spiritual needs. In fact, the group experience often attracts a new class member before the spiritual enrichment. (For more background on adult classes see chapter 1.)

Whom shall we target?

Church growth experts tell us that very few new adult class members come from within the current church membership. In fact, today's Baby Boomers usually become involved in Sunday school classes even before they join the church. So current members of the church are the least likely prospects for a new class. You will want to target new members and potential members in the community. However, you might consider both church members and non-church members who fall into these categories:

Adults are most receptive and responsive to the message of God's love when they:

- are getting married.
- decide to remain single.
- are expecting or at the birth of their first child.
- adopt a child.
- experience a miscarriage.
- separate or divorce.
- remarry.
- experience a mid-life crisis.
- experience illness.
- encounter death or another loss.
- change careers.
- encounter serious stress.
- are moving.
- lose their jobs.
- retire.
- are a victim of crime or a tragedy.
- have a religious experience.[1]

What type of class?

Some adults learn best by discussion, and lecture classes bore them. Other adults learn by lecture, and discussion classes intimidate them. Some classes may incorporate both. Some classes prefer to study a specific book of the Bible. These might be called *Bible-centered* classes. However, it is important to have at least one class in the church that is *life-centered,* studying life issues and including Bible references in the teaching. This type of class often attracts middle age to young adults. Life-centered classes act as entry points for Baby Boomers and Generation Xers who have very little experience with the Bible. These adults fear appearing ignorant in a Bible-centered class. It is important for churches to offer at least two adult classes, so that adults may have a choice in subjects and learning methods.

Every church in today's society needs to occasionally offer a basic Bible 101 type class, advertised as a beginner/refresher course. This would include an overall view of the Bible;

the authors, circumstances and backgrounds under which different books of the Bible were written; exactly what the different parts of a Bible reference mean; permission to use the table of contents; methods for finding the books of the Bible without memorization (see "Getting Into The Bible" in the Appendix); and a brief history on the canonization, translations, and printing of the Bible.

What shall we name the class?

Often we pass off the name of the class as unimportant. However, the name brings about pride for class members and tells outsiders a little about the class itself.

The class name should reflect the character of the class, the struggles or joys of its members, or the study type. Do not rush naming the class, but simply call it a new class as you organize. Assist the members in selecting the name by discovering what the members want from their class experience and looking at potential names:

Acts

Agape

Alleluia

Alpha and Omega

Asbury

Bereans (see Acts 17)

Builders

Caring Class

Challengers

Choir Class

Christians in Action (CIA)

Christians in Love (CIL)

Christians Under Construction (CUC)

College, Career and Fellowship

Contemporary

Covenant

Crosstalk

Discovery

Disciples

Emmaus

Explorers

Families in Faith

Faith Roots

Faith Mates

Fellowship

Friendship

Genesis

Gospel

Ichthus

Inquirers

JOY (Jesus, Others, Yourself)

Jubilee

Koinonia

Light Shine

Living and Loving in Faith

Logos (Greek for *the Word*)

New Life Class

New Ventures

Open Door/Circle

Outreach

Pathfinders

Praise

Reachers

Reapers

Roots of Faith

SALT (Single Adults Learning Together)

Searchers

Seekers

Trinity

'Tween Friends

Upper Room

Wesley

Steps to take

Churches have used many formats in forming new adult classes. Each church is individual, and what works in one case may not work in another. See chapter 5 for class leader and officer guidelines.

Develop a plan for establishing the new class. I've found the plan below most effective in churches where I have worked. Use some of these suggestions and work out your own plan. Be flexible to adjust and adapt your plan as needed. The one constant for any plan includes prayer. A class not built on prayer lacks the strong foundation Jesus spoke of in his parable about houses built on rock and sand.

NEW CLASS STEPS

1) Begin by praying personally, and ask another person in the church to act as a prayer partner for the class. This person will probably not be a potential class member, but someone who recognizes the need for the new class. Throughout the process, keep him or her informed of the progress.

2) Ascertain which adults you wish to target. Find out all you can about the particular adults and their needs. Are they Baby Boomers? Generation Xers? (See the end of chapter 3 for information on identifying adults.)

3) Ask a good teacher to agree to a two or three month teaching commitment on subjects that will interest the particular persons you wish to attract. Leave the final selection of subjects to the class organizers. When making a teacher choice, keep in mind the target adults and their interests and preference of learning methods.

4) Approach six to eight persons (or three or four couples) to act as a core group. These persons may have expressed an interest in a new class or may be persons whom you feel are in the "category" of adults you wish to target. Ask them to pray about whether God is calling them to assist in the formation of this new class. Propose that they give a one to two year commitment as class organizers in order to get the class off the ground. If they already belong to an adult class, offer them the option to return to their present class after they complete their commitment with the new class.

Explain that you already have a teacher lined up for the first two to three months. After that time the class members will decide whether they want a regular teacher (and who it might be), or whether they want to draw teaching talent from their own class. During the first two to three months they will not have to worry about the teaching except to give the teacher some input on the subject matter. This will free the core group to work on building community in the class.

Tell the core group about its prayer partner, and introduce them if necessary. Explain that they may ask the prayer partner for specific prayers at any time.

5) With your core group, pray about and develop a list of possible contacts. Plan a beginning date, classroom location (if you have a choice!), and an introductory social. The social may be on an evening or during the Sunday school hour, depending on

---

which time the group believes would be most successful. During the social, have a very brief devotional with an introduction of your beginning subject matter, but devote most of the time to food, fellowship, and planned activities that help persons to get acquainted. Be sure that your teacher is a part of this fellowship.

6) Publicize, publicize, publicize! You and the core group will ask people through personal contact and publicize in every method possible. (See chapter 8.) Make the first class time a real red-letter day for the whole congregation. Celebrate the beginning of the new class throughout the church.

CHAPTER 5

Guiding
Leaders and Officers

Leadership in an adult Sunday school class seldom receives the prominence that it should. Much of the "glue" that holds a class together and gives it strength comes from the officers or leaders.

God calls many of us into leadership as part of our vocation. As Christians, we should distinguish between our careers and our vocations. We engage in our careers in order to make a living. As we follow God's call throughout the whole of our lives we carve out our vocations. Our vocation includes our relationships with family, our attitudes toward others with whom we work, and even those along the highways and roadways as we commute to work. For many of us, vocation includes leadership in an adult class. When we truly consider our responsibility in class a part of God's call, we carry out those responsibilities with joy and fulfillment.

Recognize your own leadership as a call from God and help others to acknowledge this calling for all class leaders. When the class recognizes the importance of these positions, persons are more likely to respond affirmatively when asked to take leadership. Without this type of dedication, the class becomes just another organization to gobble up time.

Leadership Questions

As a leader, you will be called on to guide the class in making many decisions. After assessing the decisions reflect on these questions and then involve everyone in the process:

1. What commitments, experiences, and vision do I (the leader) bring to this situation?
2. What are the values, experiences, and visions of the people with whom I work? How do their commitments interact with the situation?
3. What is the context within which I work? What commitments, limitations, and openings for ministry are present in the context?
4. What is God's call to us in this situation? Seek to discern this with the community.[1]

Guidelines for classes

All classes do not need specific bylaws, but it is a good idea for every class to adopt some sort of guidelines and print them up for class members. Here are some suggestions:

Name: State the name of the class. Give information about the meaning of the name.

Purpose: Develop a purpose statement. This might include enrichment, fellowship, support, and service.

Relationship to church: State your class's full cooperation, encouraging attendance at services and promoting full membership. Make some reference to your class's relationship to other ages rather than operating as a separate unit.

Relationship to adult council: Most adult classes are represented on an adult council by one teacher and one officer. The adult council is not a policy making group, but operates to develop awareness of adult needs within the church. These needs are passed on to policy making groups, and the adult council helps to carry out decisions and policies made for adults in the church.

Membership: By stating in printed form the fact that your class is open to any persons desiring to join, you recognize God's unlimited love for everyone.

Print your policy about placement on an inactive list if a person does not attend for a set amount of time (after contact has been made to discover the reason for non-attendance and after encouraging a person to return to active status).

Include a statement that members who are present but engaged in other Sunday school activities are kept on the active roll and informed of class activities. These last two statements will prompt you to keep a more mindful eye on your class members and their needs.

Meetings: State the "designated place" of meeting and the gathering time. You might include the usual schedule for your sessions, but leave an option for flexibility here.

Include a set time for your regular business meeting(s), even if you only state that a business meeting will be held in a specific month for election of officers. Include information on the number needed for a quorum or number required to carry a motion.

Officers: (See suggestions for officers and duties on the following pages as well as the forms "Meeting Plan Sheet" and "Summary-of-Action Form" in the appendix.) In your guidelines, state the length of time an officer will serve and the month of election. This sets parameters for the responsibility.

Include your process of nomination. It is a good policy to appoint a nominations committee for the next year at the time of elections. This committee then is alert to leadership potential throughout the year. The committee nominations, as well as nominations from the floor, are then voted on. If nominations and election take place at the time you select church leadership, then persons have a clear knowledge of their overall relationship and commitment to the church. A November or December election with a January installation fits best into most church leadership schedules.

Include your method for filling leadership vacancies and for any carry over responsibilities. Some classes create good continuity of leadership by having the vice president move into the presidency or vice versa. A split election also provides continuity. To do this, elect half of the officers at one time and the other half six months later.

Teachers: Include a statement about whether your teachers will be elected or will volunteer from the class. Check on your church's policy on approval of teachers. By stating a length of term, both teacher and class have opportunity for change.

You might want to include a statement about frequency of teachers from outside the class. Here again, recognize that your church policy probably requires that teachers come from within the church unless cleared through the church staff.

If your teachers rotate leadership, encourage rotation in blocks of weeks so that there is continuity from one Sunday to the next.

Executive Committee: An executive committee can get together much easier than the total class leadership team. State the composition of such a committee, the frequency of its meetings, and its responsibilities (such as budget, periodic review, approval of activities, etc.).

Committees: (See suggested committees with officer list on the following pages.) State whether the committee chairpersons and membership are elected or appointed and if appointed, by whom.

Finance: Some classes only collect money to cover coffee and get well cards. Other classes raise larger amounts of money to sponsor a mission or some other project. By establishing a budget in your class, you model stewardship. A budget helps us visualize a plan for the use of our gifts from God, no matter how small or extensive that budget. Set a specific time each year for review and approval of the budget. State any policy on special collections.

Recognize your class as a part of the total ministry of the church. Support it financially and with your prayers and actions. Many classes maintain their own checking account with a percentage of their offering designated for the general church account. It is important that your class contribute to the general church budget in order to affirm your support of the church. (Because of fluctuating attendance, a percentage is recommended rather than a set amount.)

Expressions of appreciation, sympathy, and so on: State occasions for such expressions and how your class will acknowledge those occasions.

Guidelines for establishing officers

The adult class officers are important leaders in the ministry of the church. Their responsibilities interrelate with other areas of the church family. Without their dedication, the educational process for all ages within the church would suffer. For this reason it is recommended that adult class officers indicate their commitment by becoming members of the church.

The size of an adult class affects not only the number of officers needed in the class, but also the policy making functions of the executive committee. A class needs to decide which positions are elected, which are appointed, and which will be members of the executive committee.

If your church does not offer help and training opportunities for the officers, organize training yourself. (See chapter 11) Such training not only provides continuity from one year to the next, but also recognizes the importance of these positions.

Another way to assist in constancy is to develop a file for each leadership position that is passed on from one person to another. The file would include a job description for that particular responsibility plus any notes and records from past years.

Recognize God's call to these leadership responsibilities by using a dedication service such as the one at the end of this chapter. Throughout the year, ask for God's guidance as the leaders carry out Christ's ministry through your class.

Here are some of the responsibilities your class may wish to recognize and suggestions for which officers might carry out those responsibilities. Use the list to evaluate or establish positions. Write up a statement of duties for your officers to use as a guideline as they carry out their jobs. Also, establish which decisions may be carried out by the executive committee and which should be brought before the class membership at large.

DUTIES:	MAY BE CARRIED OUT BY:
Overall administrative functions of the class, including programs, fellowships, and outreach. Representative to adult council. Appoints committee chairs and assists in selecting committee members.	**President**
Assists president when called on. Is responsible for securing teachers or other learning leadership. Leads in planning the program year in advance.	**Vice President (or) Program Chairperson**
Maintains class roster, updating it and printing a copy for each class member at least annually with a quarterly supplement. Maintains a weekly attendance record. Records minutes of each business or special meeting.	**Secretary**
Responsible for collection of offering, weekly percentage of offering being placed in envelope with weekly report on outside of envelope, and offering being ready for collection at appointed time.	**Treasurer (or) Secretary**
Keeps record of all monies, making deposits in class account and writing checks (working with president on expenditures). Gives a financial report at designated meetings or when requested.	**Treasurer**
Maintains a card file on each member: name, address, home and business phone, date joined class, church membership, occupation, birthday, anniversary, family members, interests, and past responsibilities in class.	**Membership Secretary/ Chairperson**
Responsible for class bulletin boards, name tags, greeters, rotating list of coffee-makers, and inventory of supplies.	**Membership (or) Sunshine**

Conducts class routine correspondence.

Corresponding Secretary

Responsible for secretarial duties for births, illnesses, class member and family deaths, helping-hand dinners, etc.

Membership (or) Sunshine (or) Corresponding Secretary

Organizes class socials, small group dinners, retreats, and outings.

Fellowship Coordinator (or) Social Chairperson

Maintains liaison between church/community and class, promoting and coordinating class members' ministry in such projects as selected by class.

Outreach Coordinator (or) Projects Chairperson (or) Welfare

Works with the education department in coordinating class members who serve elsewhere during the class time, keeping them informed of class activities and keeping the class informed of their ministry. On occasion may audio or video tape a class lesson for the members outside classroom.

Liaison to Members Outside Classroom

Responsible for devotional/prayer time each Sunday morning. (If prayer is included in the teaching plans, such a position is not necessary. However, short devotionals give leadership responsibilities and training to persons who are hesitant about teaching.)

Devotions/Prayer Coordinator

Responsible for daily ongoing prayer requests, maintaining a prayer chain of class members who agree to spend time daily praying for the class and other needs as they are identified.

Prayer Chain Coordinator

Responsible for notices in the church newsletter or bulletin, local newspaper, and other means of publicizing the class functions. (See chapter 8.) Publish a class newsletter on a routine basis.

Publicity Chairperson

Other responsibilities to be considered in assignment of duties:

Ways and means
Classroom maintenance

Telephone coordinator
Music coordinator

Review the "Meeting Plan Sheet" in the appendix. This will help your leadership keep track of the progress of meetings and give direction for any followup of decisions. There are several forms in the appendix that will help chairpersons of social events or other events to plan and carry out their functions.

Each officer or leader in the class should take the responsibility of creating an environment that nurtures members and encourages spiritual growth. At least once a year, use some sort of evaluation process to determine the future direction for your class. The "Adult Study Interest Survey" in the appendix may be helpful here.

Litany of Dedication for Officers

Leader: Each of us has different gifts.

PEOPLE: **But the same spirit gives these gifts to all.**

Leader: We use our gifts to serve God and to achieve God's purpose.

PEOPLE: **It is the same God that we all serve.**

Leader: These leaders have been called by God to help our class to grow and serve Christ's church in special ways this year.

Officers: We accept this call to ministry through _____ Class. Your support indicates your trust in us, and we place our trust in God as we fulfill our obligations.

PEOPLE: **We support these leaders as they make decisions and as they assist us in our ministry.**

Leader: These leaders need guidance as they carry out their calling.

PEOPLE: **We pledge to pray that God guide our leaders.**

Officers: With your help, O God, we begin this new opportunity for ministry in your name.

PEOPLE: **With your help, O God, our class reaches out to serve you in the ways that you direct us. Amen.**

CHAPTER 6

Teaching Tools

Some persons seem to be born teachers and others gently move into the role. Teachers can be viewed as co-learners. The need to teach extends far beyond simply passing on knowledge. But rather we teach:

- to learn and to share our learnings.
- because human beings hunger for connectedness.
- because we have experienced God's news.
- in order to search for truth, wholeness, and justice.[1]

Examine your motives for teaching. Do they parallel these? If so, then we must be co-learners in our teaching.

Teaching and learning are *not* one and the same. We may sit in a classroom for a full year, listening to a teacher, yet have very little actual learning take place. Another time we may learn something without a teacher even present. We can also learn from our mistakes, if we allow the learning to take place. Learning involves change. We can receive mountains of information and be able to recite the information back, but unless we change our direction or have new insights into the direction in which we have been going, then no actual learning has taken place. True learning brings about action, in one form or another.

Teaching can be informational or formational. One is no more important than the other. Likewise, each benefits from the other. A good blend of the two creates the best learning environment. Informational teaching simply passes on information, telling the student *about* the Bible or *about* some subject. Formational teaching gets the student *involved* with the scripture or the dilemma. One stands on the outside and looks in, and the other crawls into the scripture or the subject and actually experiences it.

Adults come to us from varied experiences and backgrounds. These experiences influence their lives and the way that each looks at himself or herself. Most adults consider themselves mature and quite reasonable. Consequently they want to make their own decisions and to be treated as independent persons.

Getting to know your students

Persons are of more value than the information to be learned. You may teach all sorts of factual information, and the student may spout it right back to you, but unless it has value to the person and makes a difference in his or her life, it is as "a noisy gong or a clanging cymbal."

Because God created us in community, to live in relationship with one another, we grow in our faith through community with others. The better you know your students, the easier it will become to prepare for your teaching and to know how you can help them.

The section "Identifying Adults" in chapter 3 will help you to understand the adults we teach. You may also want to use the "Adult Class Information Survey" in the appendix.

Some teachers keep card files on their students. I find it helpful to keep two class lists or church directories. One I use as a directory, and in the other I jot down comments and information beside the names that help me know each person better. For example, I may overhear someone comment on his struggle over his father's death last year. This information may help me direct some questions in a future study, and as I familiarize myself with resources, I may find something that I can pass on to that person.

You will gain most of your insights by listening. Every opportunity you have, listen to conversations between adults. Encourage their involvement by asking, "How do you feel about that?" or "What would you have done in that situation?" Glean insights from conversations overheard.

Don't overlook class social experiences and opportunities in the community that will give you insight into the needs, problems, and joys of your students. When you work with class members on mission tasks, when you visit together in the grocery aisle, or when you sit beside class members at a ball game, you will learn about them and they will see your message as pertinent to everyday life.

Use every opportunity to become better acquainted with your students. Use Jesus' example. In Mark 7:5-23 Jesus adapted his teaching to the Pharisees and scribes, speaking of things they would understand. In Luke 7:1-10 Jesus listened closely to the centurion, and he found a positive faith. In Matthew 15:21-28 Jesus not only listened, but he weighed the circumstances and adjusted to the needs of the woman who wished to learn. Can we learn how to be a teacher from any better teacher than Jesus?

Forming good questions and answers

Jesus taught with questions. He asked the listener's opinion in Luke 13:10-17, and in Mark 11:27-33 he responded to a question by turning a question back to the inquirer. Both of these spurred thought for the learner. In Luke 10:25-30 Jesus used a question to lead into a story.

Questions work as tools to motivate thought in your students. They may be used to introduce a subject, after reading printed material, after a presentation, or to encourage discussion about a subject. Christian education focuses on helping persons learn *how* to think rather than *what* to think. Through questions you may motivate students to think on their own, help them clarify values and make choices, encourage their own brainstorming and interpretation, and help them move toward a commitment. Remember that a teacher only creates the atmosphere. The Holy Spirit brings about the transformation.

TYPES OF QUESTIONS

Use Luke 22 as an example.

Remember
To bring to mind specific information.
Example: What Hebrew meal did Jesus eat with his disciples?

Classify
To compare or contrast data, or perhaps to describe.
Example: What mileage in our city compares with the distance that Jesus traveled from Bethany to Jerusalem during Holy Week?

Investigate
To consider explanations or reasons for action or a specific situation. This type of question asks "What do you think?"
Example: Why do you think Judas arranged for the officials to arrest Jesus?

Assess
To draw connections and conclusions, to evaluate, and to make choices. These questions encourage personal expression.
Example: Considering Jesus' cleansing of the Temple, should we sell items in the church?

Speculate
To suppose and identify possibilities of an outcome or situation.
Example: What would you have done if you had been a follower of Jesus and came upon a crowd in the street, only to discover that they were watching Jesus carry the cross?

AVOID YES/NO ANSWERS

Example: Do you think that Judas thought Jesus would allow the officials to kill him?

Reworded to encourage discussion: *What do you suppose Judas thought Jesus would do when the officials came to arrest him?*

Teaching with discussion

There is a myth that group discussion is always better than lecture. Dick Murray suggests "while some group discussion can be very stimulating, other class discussions utilize little information and consume a lot of time in opinion swapping. Discussion can also become very manipulative as it tries strongly to persuade divergent points of view to agree with the majority. Some types of personality flourish on discussion, other, quiet persons do not."[2]

This warns us to prepare for discussion as carefully as we prepare for a lecture. It also points out the importance of keeping discussion groups small, even as small as two to four persons. This gives every person opportunity to express an opinion. In large groups, certain people tend to monopolize the discussion.

Prepare questions that will move the discussion in a logical progression so as to cover the subject and keep the participants on track. As suggested in the chart above, questions need to be formed in such a manner that they require more than a yes or no answer.

Recognize that discussion takes time. If there are six persons in a group, and each person takes two minutes for a response to the question, you will use twelve minutes. If you break the class into smaller groups, set a time limit and remind them about halfway through to be sure that everyone has an opportunity to participate. This gives the group permission to ask anyone who monopolizes the conversation to finish so that others may have a turn.

Some persons process their thoughts *as* they talk while others must form their thoughts in their minds *before* they speak. Recognize this, and do not be concerned about brief silences. Silences actually invite persons to original thoughts. What seems like a long silence usually only lasts two to five seconds. Don't rush to answer your own question, because the class will come to expect this. If you receive absolutely no response, you might suggest that you may not be phrasing your question correctly and ask if someone will share with the class what he or she hears you saying. If silences are typical in your class, make it a practice to suggest that everyone think about the question silently for a minute and then give the signal for discussion to begin.

A good discussion leader must also be a good listener. You must be sensitive to feelings as well as to words, watching for body language and tone of voice. Good eye contact signals that you are listening. An occasional nod or a brief word or two also indicates your interest. Be aware that your listening stops when you begin forming words in your mind for your own response.

Any time we encourage independent thinking we will find differences of opinion. If the differences cause a conflict, simply state, "I think there is a difference of opinion here. I hear you say _____, and I hear you say _____. We can agree to disagree agreeably and move on." Indicate acceptance of all persons, even when there is a difference in opinions and ideas. When summarizing what has been said, avoid any evaluation or judgment.

A good discussion leader must keep a close watch on the time. It is as important for discussions to have a good closure as it is for lectures. You will probably need five minutes or so for this. If representatives from different groups are to give insights gleaned in their groups, then you will need more time.

Teaching in groups

Groups involve many sets of interpersonal relationships. A group of three involves six relationships, and when you increase that group by one you double the number of relationships. Consequently, the larger the number in a group, the more involved the relationships and the less time everyone has to strengthen those relationships. Since most teachers use groups for discussion at various times during a session, be sure to read the information on discussion found elsewhere in this chapter.

Brainstorming is one way to involve groups. Some call this popcorning. Students feed ideas to the leader, one right after another. The leader may list the ideas under separate headings as the ideas pop up, or they may simply be listed and then categorized later. The latter method usually keeps the brainstorming more active, suggesting that any ideas be listed, no matter how ridiculous. Avoid evaluating the ideas at this point. As you categorize the ideas later on, you may recognize that one idea is the same as or can be combined with another, or that an idea does not fit the subject after all. Allow these observations to come from the group.

Small discussion groups are the most common in Sunday school classes. The teacher must be clear about the assignment, since each group works independently. It helps for the teacher to float among the groups, available for questions if the assignment is unclear. Announce the amount of time available ahead of time, notify the groups halfway through the allowed time, and then give a warning two minutes before the time is up so that groups may conclude their conversations. These groups may or may not report back to the total class. If they report back, summarize the findings of all the groups. If they don't report back, give a closure statement about what they've discussed and move on.

The easiest way to break a class into groups for discussion is to simply ask everyone to talk with two or three persons nearby. Survey the room to be sure that everyone is included in a group. If there are some loners, ask the class to look around and be sure that no one is excluded. At times, you might add a requirement that they not be in a group with someone that they know well.

If you want to assign group members ahead of time, cut out small squares of colored paper and tape a square under each chair. Then when you want the class to divide into groups, ask them to check under their chairs for the color and get together with other persons with the same color. You may also divide them by birth months, favorite seasons, etc.

Experiential learning groups increase the number of adults who actually experience the learning. This group formation might be used with a number of experiential learning activities: reflections on flat pictures or symbols, creating an object, role playing, paraphrasing, poetry writing, or poster making. These are then shared with the class. (See "Learning Activities" below.)

Symposiums or panel dialogues include authorities or persons who have made themselves knowledgeable about a subject. After the authorities present their ideas, questions from the group may lead into a group process as discussion continues between the leaders and group participants. At times such a presentation involves dialogue between several of the authorities before or in between group participation sessions.

There are far more ways to teach in groups than we have space to mention here. For more suggestions, read *40 Ways to Teach in Groups* by Martha Leypoldt.

Teaching Bible skills and memorization to adults

Many adults today suffer from Bible naiveté. I used the word naiveté here because their lack of knowledge usually stems from a lack of experience. They may have attended Sunday school as a child, but they never used the Bible with regularity and have done almost no Bible study as an adult.

One church in Florida decided to offer a six-week Bible 101 course. They gave a brief announcement in the bulletin and newsletter, describing it as a beginner or refresher course. The teacher expected perhaps fifteen people, but sixty persons showed up at the first session. Some who responded were the elected church leaders. No wonder adults shy away from classes that center on Bible study! We adults avoid embarrassment whenever possible.

If your class is not comfortable with using the Bible, you may want to plan a refresher course. Several introductory Bible courses are now on the market, although I have yet to find one that contains such simple information as the meaning of numbers and colons in a Bible reference. You may want to create your own by using information in the front of study Bibles, suggestions in children's introductory curriculum, and Bible dictionary data. Be sure to include the history of how the Bible took shape and came to us.

For a quick refresher for your class, walk them through "Getting Into the Bible" in the appendix. Remind them that the more they use the Bible the more comfortable they will be with it. Suggest that they purchase a "working" Bible that can be highlighted and marked with notes. This encourages them to use the book at home.

To create interest in memorizing Scripture, try these suggestions:

✓ Introduce your class to ways a passage can be useful in life.
✓ Ask class members to tell about times when a memorized passage has helped them over a hard time.
✓ Look at the Scripture in various translations, encouraging class members to choose a translation they feel comfortable with.
✓ Write the passage on colorful banners or posters.
✓ Outline the passage on chalkboard or newsprint.
✓ Explain background about the passage, such as the fact that Middle Eastern sheep learn to follow their shepherd instead of being driven and that sheep will lie down and die before they will drink from flowing water (therefore the reference to still water in the 23rd Psalm).
✓ Write the verse on the chalkboard and read it together several times. With each reading erase a word, relying on your memory as you read.
✓ Use songs or chants that repeat the verse several times.
✓ Create a litany using the verse as a response.

Memorization is not an end in itself but a means toward understanding and living our faith. When we know scripture by heart, we have a wellspring of nourishment, pumped up to us, fresh at a moment's notice.

Memorization comes from the left brain. However, we must realize that some of us function out of the right side of our brain more than the left. I'm one of those people. Give me five words to memorize and I'll either rearrange the sentence or use synonyms in the place of a word. I didn't learn the alphabet until I was in the third grade, and I've learned the books of the Bible three times but could not give them to you now if my life depended on it. Consequently I've devised other methods to compensate. I mark my Bible for easy location of my favorite verses, and I locate the Bible books by sections. (See "Getting Into the Bible" in the appendix.)

Using prayer

God calls us to communication. We label that communication prayer. Contrary to many of our childhood beliefs, prayer can happen anytime and in many forms.

The most important prayer we will ever pray as teachers is offered long before we step into the classroom. How can we expect to be God's vehicle if we are not in communication with God ourselves? Only through prayer can we grow in a personal relationship with God. If you need some structure in your prayer life, try these suggestions for awhile.

Prayer

P*repare* yourself. Find a location that is comfortable, where you will not be disturbed. Luke tells us that Jesus "would go away to lonely places, where he prayed."

R*epeat* a simple verse or prayer. Learn a short Bible verse or prayer or song. Breathe slowly for several seconds, being conscious of your breathing, and then repeat the verse or prayer, or sing the song quietly.

A*ccept* God into your heart. To do this, center into the very heart of you. Consider the part of you that feels love, that feels sadness, the part that is happy when you do for others. Then ask God to come into that part of you.

Y*ield* all that bothers you to God. Whatever is troubling you, turn it over to God. Know that God understands your problems.

E*njoy* God's presence. Just spend some time "looking and loving" God. Feel God's strength and peace.

R*eview* how you felt. Consider a prayer journal, writing down some of the feelings and thoughts that came to you as you prayed.[3]

Through prayer we can prepare to lead the adults. Pray for your preparation time. Thank God for the gift of sleep the night before you teach. God gives us the gift of sleep to prepare our bodies and minds. We also must pray for those we teach. Use the prayer calendar in the appendix to pray for the members of your class.

Include prayer in your teaching plan, and not just a routine prayer. Adults who seldom pray may feel uncomfortable, but you can ease them into prayer using some of these methods:

- Write a *prayer litany*. In a litany, one or two lines are followed by a responsive phrase repeated by the entire group. The litany grows out of personal feelings and concerns when it is written as part of the class experience. Use a central theme that relates to your study for the title.

  1) Ask the class to suggest phrases or sentences that relate to the theme. I prefer not to label this as a prayer or litany as we work on it so that they use simple language and expressions from the heart. Write their suggestions on a large piece of paper. Some phrases may be combined.
  2) Select certain phrases as responses from the whole group, or you may create a specific phrase or choose a phrase from a song that will be used each time as your response.
  3) Cut the phrases apart and arrange them in some sort of pattern.
  4) Assign specific phrases for different persons or groups of voices to read.
  5) The whole group will read or sing the responses.

Recognize that this is not a performance. In fact, preparing the litany is as much a prayer as reciting it afterwards. Through the whole experience we communicate with God.

- *Guided prayers* give persons an opportunity to reflect in a very private way. Most people need some suggestion when we ask them to pray silently. Where a memorized prayer may be compared to practicing swimming strokes on the edge of a pool, a quiet inner communication with God is like relaxing in the water and being lifted and refreshed on a hot summer day. If your class has never used a guided or meditative prayer, adapt the following suggestion to your theme.

First, I want you to make yourself comfortable and close your eyes. Try to erase all thought from your mind. Simply be conscious of your breathing in and out, in and out. (Pause)

Now, think about a favorite place where you can be quiet and alone. Look around in your mind and think about what's in this place and why it's so special. (Pause)

Next, think about yourself. Think about the part of you that brings you joy when a baby smiles or that brings tears to your eyes when a friend is sad. Think of the part of you that loves, and the part that feels great when you do something for someone else. We often call this our soul. (Pause)

Invite God to come into your soul and show God something special about yourself. Show God one positive thing about yourself. (Pause) Tell God anything you would like about yourself or about a problem you may have. (Pause)

Now, bring people who are special into your soul too. Show God something special about them. Is it a special time? Is one of them having a problem, or is your relationship with that person needing some help? (Pause) Tell God how much you love these special persons and how they feel about you. (Pause) Now, in your mind watch God's love and your love flow over these persons. (Pause) Let the thoughts of those persons fade out of your mind, but continue to love them.

For right now, simply allow God to love you. Think about how that love feels, all around you, enveloping you in warmth. Enjoy just being with God. (Pause) Continue to enjoy the love and listen to what God may say to you about yourself or your problems, or the people you love. (Pause) When you are ready you may open your eyes.

- *Use poetry* to create prayers. See the information under "Learning Activities" below.

Learning activities for adults

In a learning activity, the process creates the learning. Any finished object is simply a by-product of the true learning. Because we confuse "crafts" with learning activities, we often ignore these possibilities for adults. We only have room for a few suggestions in this book, but there are many practical books on the market filled with additional ideas. I highly recommend Dick Murray's book *Teaching the Bible to Adults and Youth* (Abingdon), for ways to help learners encounter the scripture.

Familiar symbols can be turned into learning tools. Consider using everyday items as Jesus did. Jesus spoke of the mustard seed, the leaven, and the weeds. We might use checkbooks, briefcases, seat belts and car keys. Jesus held up a coin; we can actually bring these items into the classroom as visual focuses for our lessons.

Flat pictures make good discussion points for adults. Accumulate a collection of magazine pictures that may be used for springboards of discussion on the subject of your study. Using pictures of life situations, ask the learners to select a picture that reminds them of a time they felt stressful. Pictures of nature might suggest times they feel close to God. An assortment of pictures of people can be used to ask learners to discuss just what the person(s) might be thinking or feeling. After selecting the pictures, ask learners to talk together about their pictures in small groups.

Art type activities sometimes make adults uncomfortable, but they are good learning tools if we assure the learners that we are not looking for a great finished product.

One week we walked into our adult class and found card tables and chairs set up with poster board, tape, scissors, and markers on each table. Our assignment was to build a church with the items on the table. Some groups built elaborate structures, some built buildings with open doors, some forgot to open their doors, some built buildings with tall steeples, some were simple structures, and one group simply made paper-doll people from their poster board and taped the hands of the people together to form a circle. Each group shared their church with the whole class and told a little about their conversation as they worked. Then we discussed in our groups how a church might gather the people, what they might learn together, and what they would do for others. After sharing these ideas with the class, we talked about what sort of physical upkeep a church building needs, what sort of people-upkeep a congregation needs, and what sort of people-upkeep our class uses. We recognized that relationships within the class break down when persons quit coming and we did very little to repair the breakdown.

A good way to evaluate or summarize your year is to give small groups large pieces of paper and markers and ask them to use pictures or words to tell about what they have learned during the year. With adults, encourage illustrations, even simple stick figure drawings, but assure them that words on the paper can be symbols too.

Poetry can be written in a variety of forms. Since we are not teaching an art form, but using poetry writing as a tool, the rules of poetry are not crucial. You can use poetry best by encouraging learners to simply put some thoughts on paper (or on the chalkboard if you are doing it as a group) and then begin to rearrange and restructure the sentences to form the poem.

Free verse uses various phrases, sentences, or a series of words. The lines may be any length. Remember that the learning takes place as we develop a poem, and that learning is more important than a finished product.

My favorite poetry activity with adults is the cinquain (sin cane) poem, which has five lines:

1) A one-word title or the subject.
2) Two words that tell something about the subject. They may be separate words or words in a phrase.
3) Three action words or a phrase about the subject. These are often verbs or "ing" words.
4) Four "feeling" words about the subject. This may also be a phrase about how the subject feels or how you feel about the subject.

5) The subject word again or another word with the same meaning. Or if this is a prayer poem, you may want to use Amen here.

Creation

Power   Majesty

Moving   Growing   Enriching

Active: then, now, forever

God

Journaling time may be a good experience for your class, particularly if it is small. Give each adult a blank notebook and provide pens. Set aside some personal time each week for them to spend time in personal reflection. During the first weeks you may suggest that they recall ways that they have seen God at work during the week or ways that they will allow God to work through them in the upcoming week. During the year you may suggest other reflection themes, but tell them that the books are their personal journal and confidential. This time should be routine, at the beginning or close of the class, and the books kept in a secure place and brought out each week. At the end of the year they will take them home as a record of how their faith has grown during the year.

Retelling the Bible story can be done by paraphrase (using their own words) or telling the story from the point of view of one of the characters in the story. This may be done verbally or in writing.

The five senses make powerful tools for learning. You might bring objects into the room for the learners to see, hear, smell, touch or taste, or you may simply ask them to imagine such senses as you read the Bible passage or tell the story. For example, ask the class to imagine a place with pens of sheep and cages of doves. Add to that scene the loud voices of the merchants, calling to persons as they enter the temple courtyard. Ask the class how such an area might sound; how it might smell; and what sort of influence it might have on someone coming to worship. Then read the story of Jesus' driving the money changers from the temple. Allow persons to discuss in small groups of two or three how they felt about the sensory experience.

Drama or role play is popular with children and youth, but we seldom recognize how it may be used with adults. In a role play learners are asked to put themselves in the place of a person in a story or to finish an open-ended story about a dilemma. These may be assigned in a unique fashion by writing the dilemmas on cards and placing them in a fish bowl. A person (or team) then draws a card from the bowl, reads it out loud, and finishes the statement "What would you do if . . . ?"

Narration drama is effective when a person strolls into the classroom, dressed as the primary character in a story or as a bystander, and proceeds to tell the story as if it happened to him or her.

Volunteers may be asked to sit before the class for a play reading. This requires no preparation or props, and the volunteers simply read the parts of specific characters as they come up.

The teacher of our adult class put a new twist into our story one morning. We walked into class and she asked for four volunteers to come up front. She sat them each on a high stool. Then she began to tell the Parable of the Good Samaritan, although she did not give us the name of the story. She explained that a man was walking through a very risky area, and he was afraid for his safety. She then asked the first volunteer what that man might be seeing and how he might feel. She asked him to use the first person to tell about it. Next she explained that sure enough, some of the man's worst fears came about. He was beaten and robbed and left on the sidewalk to die. She asked the first volunteer to explain how the man might feel then. After his explanation she continued the story, saying that the pastor of a nearby church happened to pass by on the way to the city hall, late for a meeting about approval of the new building site. The pastor saw the beaten man and walked across the street to avoid him. The teacher then asked the second volunteer to explain just what the pastor might be thinking and feeling. Then the teacher told of a church official who next encountered the beaten man and passed by on the other side of the street. The third volunteer was asked to comment on the church official's feelings. Finally, the teacher told us that a person from another country who could scarcely speak English came upon the beaten person, and he stopped and cared for his wounds and called 911. Since the robbers had taken the man's credit cards and even his ID papers, the foreigner offered to pay for the man's hospital care. The teacher then asked the fourth volunteer to explain how the foreigner might feel. Finally, the teacher asked the first volunteer to make any comments he might give to a reporter once he had recovered from the ordeal.

Don't rule out any form of drama simply because you are teaching adults. Be creative about ways that you can adapt the drama to adults.

Adapting curriculum to your class

It is essential that we recognize that the central goal in teaching is the goal of helping our learners develop their own relationship with God and live out God's call in their lives. Evaluation of any printed curriculum and adjustment you make to that plan must fulfill that goal. Be sure to read chapter 7, *Planning Resources,* as you consider curriculum.

It is of primary importance that you know your students when you select or adapt curriculum. You will need to know their reading levels (and don't assume that all adults read rapidly or at a high school level) and their spiritual formation. If your class acts as an entry point for persons who have spent little or no time in church, then you know that an in depth theological study on euthanasia will scare many of them away. They may be more likely to appreciate a study on how to cope with stress. Senior adults may not be interested in a study on raising children in a Christian home, but you may be able to take materials from that curriculum and give them ways that they can contribute to the spirituality of their grandchildren.

Curriculum authors must write for teachers from many backgrounds and experiences. As a new teacher, you may feel more comfortable following the printed suggestions rather closely. However, you will need to appraise the amount of time available and your class interests, and at times you may choose to leave out an activity or substitute another. It is important, however, that the goals of the lesson be carried out in any adjustment that you make to the curriculum.

Writing your own lesson plans

Writing your own lesson plans properly takes a considerable amount of time. Before you spend that time, be sure that the subject you want to cover is not already available in printed curriculum. Publishers now recognize the vast interests of today's adults and offer many more subjects than in the past. You may have to look at specific lesson titles within a given piece of curriculum to find just what you need, but it's usually worth the search. Consult someone in your church who has a wide knowledge of curriculum. If no one in your church has this experience, call your publishing company and ask their advice.

If you develop your own lesson plan often, you will begin to develop a pattern that works for you. In the meantime, you may begin with these steps that I find helpful. You will find a form for a lesson plan in the appendix. Use it to keep you on track.

Steps for Creating Lesson Plans

1) Pray for guidance.
2) Read and review all resources (books, articles, videos, Bible, etc.).
3) Ask yourself, "What is the main idea or thought that I want to get across?" Write it in your own words.
4) Think about the individual students in your class. Get out your list and consider each person prayerfully.
5) Ask yourself, "How do I want the learners to experience the main idea?" Use action words to write these experiences, such as "hear," "discuss," "act out."
6) Plan any presentation you (or someone else) will give.
7) Make lists of materials you will need, special room arrangements, who else will be responsible for what and whether they have been contacted, and any additional preparation necessary.
8) Practice telling any stories or presenting any materials.
9) Pray for God to use you as a tool for the adults' learning.

ENJOY THE SESSION

10) Take time to debrief and take stock of how the session went. For suggestions on this, see the section below on evaluation.

Evaluating sessions

We shy away from the Big E word—EVALUATION! Actually, we do better to think of this as a debriefing experience. Our goal in evaluation is to take an objective look at what went on during the class time and become a better teacher because of it. As you consider the experience, use these questions:

- What were some of the positive things that happened during the session?
- What were some of the trouble spots? Were they things I could have avoided ahead of time? How else might I have handled the situation?
- What evidence of growth did I see in individuals?
- Who asked questions that went unanswered or in some other way expressed a need for some followup? How might I help that person?

- Did we reach the goals? If not, why? Were the goals attainable?
- How did the room arrangement contribute to the success or failure of the session?
- What reaction did the students have to the activities? Would I want to use them again in another situation? Do they need some adjusting?
- Did I overlook something in my preplanning?
- How can I improve in the future?

CHAPTER 7

Planning Resources

At the end of class the president announced, "Next Sunday, since no one volunteered to teach, we'll spend the time discussing just what you want to study for the next quarter. So bring your ideas!" As the class disbanded, I heard a couple of comments that set me to thinking.

"Well, next week will be a waste of time! I really don't know what I want to study, just something that helps me get through tomorrow!"

"I don't want to volunteer an idea because I'm afraid they'll ask me to teach it. Maybe I'll be sick next week!"

Some adults have no interest in deciding just what they will study. However, other adults may want some input into such decisions, particularly middle age and younger adults. These adults don't want to waste their time on study irrelevant to their lives, and it is important that the subject meet their needs.

Asking a whole class to plan for curriculum is risky business. In the first place, it takes time to put together purpose statements, goals, and a cohesive plan—more time than one morning of general discussion. By throwing it open to everyone in the class, you also run a chance of hodgepodge lessons with no real design.

If your class uses a dated denominational curriculum, the denomination has thought through your study outline, and you are probably skimming this chapter. For classes that use a variety of books and curricula, it is important that you come up with a firm plan. To design your studies I suggest a small committee with verbal and written input from class members. The chair of the committee needs to have good organizational and people skills in order to keep the group on task. It helps for the chair to be knowledgeable about available materials, but another resource person can easily serve in this capacity.

Select the committee by recognizing persons who know and care about other members of the class and who exhibit creativity. Ask them personally, pointing out how their gifts of caring and creativity will enhance the class through this ministry. If the class has a regular teacher (or two or three that rotate) be sure to include them on the committee, or at least consult them about your decisions. It is important that the teacher be committed to the curriculum.

A plan of action for the curriculum committee

- Set purpose statements and goals for curriculum.
- List past subjects and curriculum used.
- Develop and conduct a written Adult Study Interest Survey. (See appendix.)

- Accumulate possible resources.
- Gather names of resource persons in your church and community.
- Look at the church calendar year for possible subjects.
- Set up a study outline for six months or a year, line up teachers or discussion leaders, and publicize upcoming subjects. (See chapter 8 for publicity.)

Set goals

The purpose statement and goals that you set will depend on your class, your church's educational goals, and your own denomination. First, study the five audiences (fellowship, traditionalists, study, social action group, and multiple interest group) discussed in chapter 3. Determine which area your class fits and recognize their characteristics and needs. Then look at any educational goals that your church and denomination have set.

Next, brainstorm words that describe ways you hope your class members will grow in the upcoming year. From those words, begin to form **purpose statements.** You might include:

- growth in biblical and theological understanding in everyday life situations.
- developing a growing knowledge of the Bible.
- developing spiritual formation and communication with God.
- appreciation for the church's history and mission.
- evidence of living the faith and sharing it with others each day.

Under the purpose statements set specific **measurable goals** such as:

- learn about the symbols found in our sanctuary.
- practice ways to mention God without sounding pious.
- recognize opportunities to worship God spontaneously.

Adult study interest survey

In order to include individual members' input into the class study plan, tailor a study interest survey. Persons feel more comfortable in answering the survey truthfully if they can answer anonymously. However, you may want to leave an option at the bottom for the name, or prepare a separate page for persons to list subjects they might consider teaching themselves.

Response to the questions may be recorded by percentages, by check marks, or by fill-in blanks. Some surveys give a line after each question or statement with points from one to ten. Indicate which end of the line is high preference and which is low, and ask the class members to mark along the line just where their interest in that subject lies. Always allow space for comments.

Use the "Adult Study Interest Survey" in the appendix or adjust the form to make it appropriate for your class.

Resource suggestions

Curriculum resources range from dated Bible studies to current videos. Check with your education department for materials stored in your church library or resource room. Your denominational district or state office may also have a list or display of available curriculum. Most denominations publish a list of dated and undated resources available for purchase. You might ask for back issues of dated curriculum for your review. Ask your education department to consider ordering a copy of one or two of the undated resources each quarter until your church has samples of all those available. This makes future curriculum decisions easier.

Plan an Adult Study Fair for your church. Gather samples of all curriculum available for your adult classes and display them on a Sunday. Include books, subject and dated curriculum, videos, audio tapes, etc. Advertise it well and suggest that all adults stop and review your resources. Assign knowledgeable persons in different areas of the display to answer questions.

Many classes enjoy reviewing current inspirational or self-help books. Some classes order the books for members to purchase and read each week in preparation for the class time. Other classes ask a teacher to read the book and present a review in two or three sessions.

When using materials not on denominational recommended lists, be sure to check with your education committee. Many churches require that all curriculum be approved by that committee. It is important that staff persons responsible for education be aware of just what you are teaching so that they can share this information with prospective class visitors. The Study Plan in the appendix may be used to provide this information.

Study calendar

We adults tend to categorize our lives. However, God calls us to our Christian walk in every area of life. Developing a study calendar with the church and national calendars in mind helps adults act out their Christian faith. Use the following dates to build themes into your study calendar. From year to year, and from church to church, some events may differ in dates or months. Also consider specific events that occur only in your church or that are one time occurrences this year. The form "Adult Class Study Outline" in the appendix may be reproduced and used by your curriculum committee.

CALENDAR SUGGESTIONS	
Month/Day	*Subjects*
JANUARY	
New Year's	Goal setting
	God's plan for my life
	Personal discipline
	Stewardship of time
Epiphany (12 days after Christmas)	Wisemen's visit
	Gift giving
January—March	Call to prayer and self-denial
Martin Luther King, Jr. Birthday	Status of minorities
	Christian heroes
	Jesus' attitude toward Gentiles

Month/Day	Subjects
Week of Prayer for Christian Unity	Other denominations; interdenominational missions; ethnic minorities
FEBRUARY	
Valentine's Day	Friendships; relationships
Human Relations Sunday	Races and cultures: alike & different
Brotherhood Week	Peace
Ash Wednesday	Repentance; reflection on Christ
Lent	Self-denial; fasting; Jesus' sacrifice
MARCH	
World Day of Prayer	Prayer
Holy Week	Events of Holy Week; events from disciples' view
Confirmation	Study of membership vows
APRIL	
Easter	Resurrection; personal renewal
Heritage Sunday	Past Christian heroes, pioneer Christianity; hymnology
Spring	God in creation
Earth Day	Stewardship of the earth
MAY	
National Family Week	Family relationships; crisis; multi-generational families; marriage, divorce, widowhood, never married
Mother's Day	Motherhood; parenthood
Festival of the Christian Home	Family devotions; communications; Christian family financial planning
Ascension Day	Christ's Ascension
Memorial Day	God and nation
Pentecost	Pentecost; early church; Peter
World Order Sunday	Peace; communication
JUNE	
Denominational conference	Structure of your denomination
Father's Day	Fatherhood; parenthood
Vacations	(See August)
JULY	
Independence Day	God and nation
Vacations	(See August)

Month/Day	Subjects
AUGUST	
Vacations	Re-creation; God's plan for leisure; stewardship of time
School begins	New beginnings; God's gift of intellect
SEPTEMBER	
Labor Day	Job versus vocation of being a Christian
Promotion and Third Grade Bibles	Evaluate personal spiritual development; how the Bible came to be; Bible study aids
Christian Education Sunday	Local Christian education opportunities; history of the Sunday School; the family as teacher; denominational foundations for teaching and learning; aims of Christian education
OCTOBER	
World Communion Sunday	Communion meaning; in other countries
Laity Sunday	Responsibility of the laity in the church; local church structure and where each person can minister; membership vows
Reformation Day	Martin Luther and the Reformation
Stewardship Campaign	Stewardship of time, talent, and resources (including environment); tithing; Christian financial planning
NOVEMBER	
All Saints' Day	Early church saints; sainthood of all believers
World Community Day	Other races/ethnic groups; world peace
Veteran's Day	Peace
Bible Sunday (National Bible Week)	How the Bible came to be; Bible study aids
Thanksgiving	Thanks to God
DECEMBER	
Advent/Christmas	Preparing for Christmas; Christmas traditions; symbols; Study Christmas stories in each gospel (or various translations) and how differ
Student Day	Student campus ministries
Watch Night (Dec. 31)	Pray/dedicate self for new year

ADDITIONAL TOPICS

- Aging
- Aging parents
- Baptism
- Bible study
- Bible background
- Correlate with children's study themes
- Covenants (Noah, Abraham, Moses/Israelites, Jesus, our covenants with God)
- Crime/Violence
- Death
- Ethnic concerns of the Christian
- Evangelism (sharing your faith/fear of sharing your faith)
- Faith in the workplace
- Faith stages
- Holy Spirit
- Human rights
- Denominational doctrinal statements
- Denominational social principles
- Health and wholeness
- Juggling/Balancing competing time demands
- Life management (career/family/lifestyle/money/success/transitions)
- Marriage (building partnership/resolving conflicts/communication/growing together in Christ/ mastering money)
- Mission studies
- Nature/creation and God
- Parenting
- Pluralism
- Prayer
- Servanthood
- Sexuality for the Christian
- Sharing faith with children
- Singles
- Spiritual gifts
- Spiritual life and/or prayer
- Stress
- Television awareness
- The environment
- Theology (developing a personal)
- Worship: What is it? Understanding parts of the service

Check your curriculum plan

Use the "Study Plan" form in the appendix to inform the education office of your studies. It is important that staff persons know what adult classes are studying. Some churches require that all curriculum or study plans be approved by the education committee.

As you complete your curriculum plan, check it against these questions:

1) Is the content of each study unit consistent with our biblical heritage?
2) Is the content of each study unit consistent with our denominational heritage?
3) Is the content of each study unit relevant to the needs and interests of the class members?
4) What difference will this study unit make in the lives of the class members?
5) Does the content of each study unit invite the class members to learn more?
6) Does the content of each unit invite the class members to enter into a personal relationship with God as known through Jesus Christ?[1]

CHAPTER 8

Publicizing Adult Classes

In our world of high technology we in the church still fail to recognize the importance of communication. Publicity covers three primary functions in an adult class:

1) Notify members of the class of upcoming events.
2) Inform the church of happenings in our class.
3) Interest persons in the community in our class.

Notify members

Sometimes Sunday school classes are so loosely organized that we just expect all members of the class to know about an event when we announce it on Sunday morning. We forget about persons out of town or sick, or persons who happen to be working in other areas of the church that particular week. We also forget that announcement times during an adult class sometimes swim on the surface of our minds and never submerge. Every class needs some sort of printed information about upcoming events, whether it be a newsletter or simple printed announcements. This can either be handed out during class time or mailed to the home. A home mailing reminds students of the class during the week and also makes a caring statement from the church.

Newsletters should be well-produced, uncluttered, and informative. Today's adults seldom read "busy material." Plan routine places for regular columns to enable quick reference: announcements of upcoming study topics, names and phone numbers of class contact persons, social events, prayer concerns, etc. Leave plenty of white space so that the newsletter does not appear cluttered. Most classes find monthly newsletters most efficient, but some work with a quarterly publication. Find someone in the class who will take the newsletter as his or her ministry, and don't burden that person with other responsibilities.

PLANNING A NEWSLETTER

Use this list to plan just what you would like in your newsletter:

Items to include:	**Regularly**	**Occasionally**
☐ Contact persons for questions about class	☐	☐
☐ Upcoming study topics	☐	☐
☐ Upcoming social events	☐	☐
☐ Prayer concerns	☐	☐
☐ Joys to share	☐	☐
☐ New class members/visitors	☐	☐
☐ Reports of projects, etc	☐	☐
☐ Seasonal	☐	☐
_____	☐	☐
_____	☐	☐
_____	☐	☐
_____	☐	☐

Telephone trees help to get the message around, particularly when something comes up between meetings. Select several calling captains who receive the information and in turn call a list of class members, thereby making contact with everyone in the class.

Inform the church

Create pride in your class! Use every opportunity you can to get your class and what you do before the whole congregation. In this way you not only publicize your class, but you encourage other classes to follow your example.

- Take pictures of persons in your class as they work on projects and display them at a central location in the church.
- Write up a report on special projects or activities for the church newsletter after the event as well as announcements before hand. Include the 5 Ws and HOW: What, when, where, who, why, and how. Add a picture to the article.
- Interview persons who work on an event and put the interview in the church newsletter. Make the interview positive, stating the satisfaction that the person receives through participating.
- Video tape a class session, project, or activity, and arrange for it to play in a central gathering place on Sunday morning.
- Place a nice sign identifying this as your class, project, or activity.
- When you sponsor church wide events, such as an Easter sunrise service or a yard sale, be sure that your class name is connected with the event.
- Create a litany in class and make arrangements for the church to use it during worship. Be sure that your class is mentioned in the bulletin or from the pulpit when the litany is announced.

- If there is a T-shirt or other form of identification with your project, decide on a specific Sunday that everyone will wear them to church and announce this in the bulletin.
- Make an eye-catching sign for your classroom door.
- Make a flyer or brochure about your class and arrange for copies to be available for new members and visitors in the church. In the flyer include:
  - ☐ Name of class
  - ☐ Time and meeting location
  - ☐ Makeup of class (wide range of ages or other characteristics)
  - ☐ Class purpose statement
  - ☐ Format (lecture, discussion, mixture of lecture and discussion)
  - ☐ Teacher(s)
  - ☐ Projects of class
  - ☐ Types and frequency of social events
  - ☐ Contact persons and phone numbers for additional information

Interest people in community

How will they know about us unless we tell them? This is simple evangelism. If we're not excited enough about our class to share it with our friends and others in the community, then it's not exciting enough for the friends to want to come. The man whom Jesus healed of leprosy was so excited that he simply could not keep quiet! (Mark 1:40-45) When our excitement spreads to others the class will grow. Soon we will have one of those "nice kinds of problems" where you have to find a larger room. Numbers aren't important, but spreading the message of Christ is!

- Encourage members to share flyers or newsletters from your class with their friends.
- Arrange for newspaper or TV coverage of mission projects that your class sponsors. This not only advertises your class, but it also witnesses to the world that Christ makes a difference in the world through you. You are more likely to have your information published if you type it double-spaced and include the 5 Ws and HOW: What, when, where, who, why, and how. Include a name and phone number in case there are questions.
- If your class sponsors smaller support groups, encourage your friends to join. This may be the first step toward involvement in the church.
- Adopt a roadway, listing your class as the sponsor. This gets your class and church name at a location where it is read many times a day.
- If a member of your class receives recognition in the paper or newsletter, make sure that the write-up includes his or her relationship to your class.
- Design special class T-shirts for class members and their families to purchase and encourage them to wear them around the community. When persons ask about the shirts, members have an opportunity to tell them about the class.

ROSWELL PRESBYTERIAN CHURCH
755 Mimosa Boulevard
Roswell, Georgia 30075
Telephone: (404) 993-6316

A Faith Community
Seeking to Extend the Love of Christ

ROOTS CLASS 1992-93

A CLASS FOR INQUIRERS, NEW, AND
PROSPECTIVE MEMBERS

Roswell Presbyterian Church
755 Mimosa Boulevard
Roswell, Georgia 30075
Telephone: (404) 993-6316

WHAT WE WILL STUDY

During the class sessions, we will study:

PRESBYTERIAN COMMITMENT AND BELIEF: We will discuss the meaning of commitment to Christian discipleship and some basic doctrines of our reformed faith. Emphasis will be given to distinctives of our Presbyterian belief. A study of the Sacraments will be included.

PRESBYTERIAN GOVERNMENT: This will be a discussion of one of the primary distinctives of the Presbyterian Church - Her church government. We will look at church government denominational-wide, as well as how the local congregation is governed.

PRESBYTERIAN HISTORY: This class will study the origins and history of the Presbyterian Church. We will also look at the beginnings and history of our historic Roswell Presbyterian Church.

WORSHIP AND WORK OF ROSWELL PRESBYTERIAN CHURCH:

- ▫ A presentation of the meaning and rationale for our form of worship.
- ▫ A look at the opportunities for study through our Sunday School and other study opportunities.
- ▫ Outreach: Explanation of the many opportunities for service in and through the church.

CALENDAR FOR THE ROOTS CLASS

Sunday - 9:45 a.m.

SEPTEMBER

13 Reception of New Members
NEW CLASS BEGINS
20 Commitment and Belief
27 Sacraments

OCTOBER

4 Presbyterian Government
11 Reception of New Members
18 History of Roswell Presbyterian Church
25 Presbyterian History

NOVEMBER

1 Worship and Work of Roswell Presbyterian Church
8 Reception of New Members
NEW CLASS BEGINS
15 Commitment and Belief
22 Sacraments and History
29 Presbyterian Government

DECEMBER

6 History of Roswell Presbyterian Church
13 Reception of New Members
20 Worship and Work of Roswell Presbyterian Church

JANUARY

10 Reception of New Members
17 Commitment and Belief
24 Sacraments
31 Presbyterian Government

FEBRUARY

7 Presbyterian History
14 Reception of New Members
21 History of Roswell Presbyterian Church
28 Worship and Work of Roswell Presbyterian Church

MARCH

14 Reception of New Members
NEW CLASS BEGINS
21 Commitment and Belief
28 Sacraments

APRIL

4 Presbyterian Government
11 Reception of New Members
18 Presbyterian History
25 History of Roswell Presbyterian Church

MAY

2 Worship and Work of Roswell Presbyterian Church
9 Reception of New Members

ROOTS CLASS

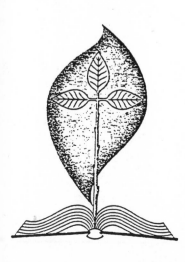

CHURCH OFFICE

SANCTUARY / EDUCATION BUILDING 'A'

Third Floor

Lower Level

Main Level

HISTORIC SANCTUARY

Basement

Main Level

Lower Level

CONGREGATIONAL LIFE BUILDING

Upper Level

Lower Level

Roswell Presbyterian
Church School Classrooms

EDUCATION BUILDING 'B'

Lower Level

Upper Level

Layout of Buildings from Mimosa Boulevard.

Where

We

Meet!

Visitors

Your attitude toward visitors in your classroom makes one of the most important statements about your class. This too is publicity, because the visitor will share the word with other folks.

Name tags are important here, not only name tags for members, but also good quality name tags for visitors. This tells visitors that they are important to you, that you want to know their name.

Followup is just as important. One adult class has an assigned person to write a letter immediately following the first visit, thanking the person for coming, telling the visitor about the class, and inviting him or her back. This letter is handwritten to make it more personal.

Be creative

Look for additional ways to creatively get the word out about your class. Print messages on balloons, print your own "Little Book of Everyday Advice" and give copies to graduating seniors, sponsor a children's class by providing teachers who get to know the parents and tell them about your class, volunteer as ushers for one Sunday wearing badges that day identifying yourselves as class members, or place books in the church library in honor of new babies and put the class name on gift plates in the books.

Pride in your class signals a pride in Christ's ministry. Who knows, some little publicity from you might make a difference in someone's life.

9

Adding Events

Laughter sounded down the corridor. Pajama-clad children ran up and down the halls, slipping into one open door and then another. A voice called from one room, "Caroline and Ashley, time to go to the babysitters now!"

It was Friday night at the State Park Lodge, the first night of the adult Sunday school class retreat. Caroline and Ashley knew they were beginning a weekend of excitement with other families from their church. Most of the children had been on their parents' retreat in past years, and they often played together at other class social events. In front of me I saw true Christian community blooming. What a heritage these children will have as they grow through their teen years, laughing, playing, worshiping, and studying with other families in their church.

Retreats

In the late 1800s and into the twentieth century, camp meetings or "encampments" were popular. Families spent a week at a campground in the woods, listening to good preaching, singing gospel songs, and visiting in each other's cabins in between. There is some resurgence of this in areas of the South today. But with so many two-career families and other demands on our time off from work, few of us can afford a week's time. Class or church wide weekend retreats are good alternatives for the Christian community-building that camp meetings offered in the past.

Select a location close enough to reach after work on Friday. If possible, extend the retreat through Sunday morning, closing with an intergenerational learning and worship experience. Some adult classes make this an annual affair on a specific weekend each fall or spring. The date has become automatic for each year's calendar, and family and work schedules are built around it. The retreat is a year-round conversation event and a highlight of the children's memories.

Consider some of the suggestions below for retreats. Plan one for your own class, or act as the host group, making the plans for the entire church. The form "Retreat Pre-Planning" in the appendix will help with your planning.

- Plan a weekend *family retreat.* Invite teenagers along to babysit the children at specific times in order to give the adults private time for study and reflection. Allow unstructured family time too, and plan at least one intergenerational learning experience that includes everyone at the retreat, teenage babysitters and families. You might also include a time when the teenagers babysit for the children and the adults have a "night on the town" at a nice restaurant.

- *Personal reflection retreats* help class members grow in their faith. Arrange for speakers on a specific theme and set time aside for private meditation.

- *A Day of Silence* was a new experience for me. In this retreat, all or most of the time is spent in silence. Periodically we came together for a brief inspirational message, sometimes given verbally and sometimes printed. Then we again went to private locations of our choosing, somewhere on the grounds.

- *Individual retreats* may be arranged at homes or camping areas. This would be an ongoing opportunity, available for persons who need time to get completely away and be alone for a day or two. Perhaps someone in your church has a vacation home or condominium that could be made available for a nominal fee. Someone in the class would be the contact person, arranging use of the facility.

- *Planning retreats* for class officers not only provide a specific framework of time for planning but also offer an opportunity for group building among the class leaders. This may be held at the church or in a home. A half day or morning and early afternoon provides a good time frame for this. Spend time evaluating the past year, planning for the next, and doing some long-term dreaming. Don't forget to build in some spiritual enrichment too.

- *Work mission retreats* combine retreat time with mission projects. See ideas for mission projects below and add some worship and community-building experiences.

Additional study experiences and support groups

The study time offered during your class will likely be sufficient for most of your class members. However, as adults mature in their faith, we need to offer additional study opportunities. Most of these opportunities should be short-term to accommodate today's busy schedules. Typically adults today avoid unending commitments to study groups, but sometimes persons in a short-term study find that they enjoy each other and have common study needs. Out of that can grow an ongoing group of a special format to study a particular subject.

Ideas listed below include one-time events, short-term studies, and ongoing study groups.

- *Visit church-sponsored agencies or church historical sites.* Write to your denominational offices for locations. You might even publish a leaflet for families to use as they travel, suggesting places that they may visit.

- *Develop support groups,* such as working parents who meet for breakfast before work or stay-at-home parents who hire a common babysitter and meet on a weekday morning. Single parents may take their families out to Sunday lunch together, or step-families may enjoy a picnic. See "Guidelines for Ongoing Support Groups" in the appendix.

- *Plan a workshop on journaling* to teach adults to reflect in this manner. Those attending the workshop may select to meet together from time to time throughout the year to exchange thoughts they have had during their private journaling time. Set a regular time for this meeting, or each time you get together decide on the time of your next meeting. About once a month is good timing for this exchange.

- *Write and publish meditations* for a specific season, such as Advent and Lent. This provides double learning: for persons who write and for persons who read the meditations.

- *Book study groups* build fellowship and enrich our lives. These should be limited to a small number of people in order to meet comfortably in homes. Such groups usually meet once a month, reading a book in between meetings, with reflective discussions during their meetings. The group's needs and interests will determine the books studied. They might deal with life skills, spiritual formation, theological concepts, mission and ministry of the church, or biblical background and understanding.

- *Develop guides for self-directed study programs* for spiritual formation, including specific books, articles, videos, and scripture. Because of their busy schedules, young and middle aged adults often prefer this sort of study. Twelve weeks is a good duration for such a study. Plan for those taking the self-directed study to meet together two or three times to share their excitement over the study. (See "Adult Self-Directed Study Form" in the appendix.)

  Persons who take a self-directed study may be encouraged to teach the subject to adult classes. Keep a roster of those who have completed the studies, and encourage them to share with classes in the future.

- *Use audio and video media for independent studies.* These may be purchased tapes or studies that your class develops and presents on tape. If your class members spend time in their automobiles commuting, audio tapes can offer study time.

- *Advertise your church library,* highlighting specific books, magazines, videos, etc. in the newsletter. Plan a library open house and present oral book reviews. Invite local authors to meet your church members and discuss their books. Take a book cart to class or set up a book table to encourage borrowing books.

- *Produce a musical or play* for the church using a seasonal theme or event. Lead the cast and supporting cast in a study on the theme before you even begin rehearsal. With this background, the production becomes more meaningful to the cast, and they in turn bring new insight to the production. Additional learning takes place if the adults actually write the script.

- *Develop a liturgical dance group or symbolic movement choir.* As the adults plan certain motions to interpret the words, they will study the meaning of the hymns or scripture.

- *Prepare booklets or post signs* to explain symbols and stained glass windows in the church. Stained glass windows were learning tools of the early church. Make banners and murals, and experiment with other graphic arts. You will learn as you prepare the art, and others will learn as they view it.

- *Seasonal workshops* for individuals or families are usually received well. These help persons center on the significance of the upcoming season. These are usually one-time events and often experiential in nature. We often overlook single persons at seasonal times when others are celebrating in families. Consider a workshop to help them cope with the holiday season.

Outreach projects

There is a new term in the schools across the country that adults need to use: service-learning. In service-learning we serve and learn, but we also develop a new lifestyle. We adults will really grow in our faith when we begin to live our life in service and at the same time turn that service into learning experiences for ourselves as well as for those we serve. The Work Camp/Mission Project Pre-planning form in the appendix will help you plan.

- *Paint or winterize a home.*

- *Help staff a soup kitchen or homeless shelter.*

- Plan a *breakfast cookout* for a home for mentally disabled adults.

- *Adopt a children's class.* Coordinate teachers from your class, pray for the class, plan a party for the class, and invite the class to share some of their songs, artwork, or drama with your class. This not only offers a ministry to the children and helps you to better appreciate the children in your church, but it also gives the children an opportunity to get to know adults other than their parents or their parents' friends.

- *Rotate as "huggers"* in preschool classes, giving children experience with other adults. Older adults can especially offer a service here, because many of the children today seldom have experience with older adults, except perhaps a week a year with grandparents.

- *Grow a garden,* using church property or a vacant lot. Arrange to give the produce to a mission agency or sell it at a reasonable price and use the proceeds for a mission project. Families can take turns tending the garden, providing family together-time experiences.

- *Glean* for the hungry. Arrange with farms, stores and restaurants to collect their excess and give it to soup kitchens or other agencies.

- *Shop* with children of single parents for their gifts for the parent.

- *Build* playgrounds, park facilities, etc. for the community or a mission agency.

- *Plant trees* at a park or along a highway, or plant trees in your church yard.

- *Clean up litter* in areas around the city. You might even adopt a road and list your class and church on the sign posted on the road.

- *Develop a transport service* for older or disabled church members

- *Provide worship tapes* for homebound members. Arrange for families to visit and deliver the tapes. Homebound persons miss contact with younger children.

- *Develop an after school program* in your church.

- *Develop a tutoring program* for children in your community. This may be staffed at the church, or you may choose to compile a list of persons willing to act as tutors and arrange private tutoring times.

- *Design a career fair* that emphasizes ways a Christian can live in ministry through specific careers

- *Develop a church plant nursery* for flowers and plants to beautify the church buildings and to give to those ill or in crisis.

- *Adopt an existing project* such as Habitat for Humanity, Hospice, or a Volunteers in Mission endeavor.

Social events

We no longer need social events just for the sake of having something to do, but we must not forget the bonding that can happen when class members get together outside of class time for fellowship. Most classes need to plan regular social events two to six times a year. Some, such as a progressive dinner, may become a tradition and enjoyed at the same time each year.

- *Fifth Sunday brunch* is a regular occurrence in many large classes. These are usually pot luck and filled with visiting and good eats! Set up the room with chairs in clusters for easy conversation. Work out some sort of signal whereby everyone moves about the room at specific times, changing groups so that they can visit with different people. You will also want to plan for a brief devotional sometime during the hour.

- *Attend a movie* together and enjoy dessert and discussion afterwards.

- *Set up "Dinners of Eight"* by asking persons interested to sign up. For a one-time event, simply assign persons to groups of eight and select a home where they can meet. Different dishes are assigned to different couples or persons sharing the meal responsibility. If you plan to have several during the year, create different groups each time. You might assign a specific topic of conversation to be discussed at some time during the meal.

- *Organize class sporting events,* such as golfing, bowling, canoeing, or softball. You might also enjoy arranging to attend a professional sporting event together. Let these be family events.

- *Enjoy pot luck meals or cookouts,* involving the whole family.

- *Swim parties* go over well in the summer. They may be at a private home or arrange to rent a pool for your class. Some classes enjoy fun with their families at a water park.

- *Plan a game night.* Ask each family to bring their favorite table game and set up games around the fellowship hall.

- *Seasonal parties* can become traditional. One of my classes enjoyed a "white elephant" gift exchange at our Christmas parties. Each year the same rubber chicken showed up, wrapped in a nice box. At another class party a pair of pink flamingos appeared in a gift exchange. For the next few years the flamingos mysteriously appeared in the yards of different class members from time to time. Such expressions of fun build community.

- *Progressive dinners* are fun if your class isn't too large. When you outgrow one home, plan to meet in one home for the appetizers and/or dessert and divide into several homes for the main course.

- *Home dedications or housewarmings* for class members who move into new homes affirm your friendships.

- *Be creative* and think of unusual social events such as a road rally, scavenger hunt, ice cream social (with time to actually churn the ice cream), soup dinners where everyone brings something for the pot and it cooks as you party, or craft demonstrations.

CHAPTER 10

Healing Sick Classes

"**H**ere," offered my friend. "You take these and see if you can do anything with them. If they stay here they'll just die." We took the gifts home with us, three poor struggling fruit trees.

As we planted the trees we discovered that the roots of one tree were still curled inward, just as it had been in the original pot several years earlier. To grow it needed to be pulled apart and stretched over a fertile ball of dirt. The leaves of all three trees were pale; some branches had no leaves at all.

After several weeks of care, one of the trees has new shoots and may even bloom this year. Another still has firm, green leaves on half of the branches. The third tree lost all its leaves, and we may have to admit that it's come to the end of its life cycle. Recognizing the symptoms of ailing trees, tending them, and acknowledging their demise are all a part of maintaining a healthy grove.

Recognizing ailing classes

Adult classes tend to operate in a self-sufficient manner. Consequently we often miss the symptoms of illness in a class. It would do us well to look for the pale leaves and inwardly curled roots of an ailing class. Do you recognize some of these symptoms in your class?

- People visit the class once and don't come back.
- Members don't know the names of persons who visited their class.
- The class rattles around in the meeting room, giving an appearance of poor attendance.
- Persons visiting the class cannot find a seat because of overcrowding. (No room to move about and meet new persons.)
- No one is responsible for contacting persons who miss several Sundays.
- There is no plan for getting together other than study time.
- Ill or grieving class members receive no calls, cards, or support from other class members.
- Class members don't know who will teach or what subject will be taught next month.
- There is no curriculum committee nor plan for lesson content.
- The class has no hands-on project outside the classroom.
- The same few people dominate a discussion, discouraging the participation of others.
- Class members argue over study matter.

Restoring health

Recognizing an ailing class is the first step toward restoring its health. Talk with class members and recognize where the class needs help. Look at some of the suggestions below.

- Integrate fellowship and study with experiential learning activities.
- Ask three to four key persons in the class to make a personal mission of establishing relationships between class members. Perhaps prepare a directory including bits of information about each person.
- Plan social opportunities for class members outside of study time.
- Plan an enrichment retreat for class members and families. Take high school students along to baby-sit young children at specific times.
- Select a hands-on mission project for your class. Consider projects even as simple as each person bringing valentines to class and then delivering them to a nursing home.
- Select a specific need within the church that persons in the class will identify with and take on the responsibility of satisfying that need.

     One class took on leadership of a mentally disabled class because a class member's child was disabled. Another class organized and produced a drive-through nativity experience each Christmas, working on it throughout the year. A class with members who had older parents living in the community planned monthly activities, transporting older adults to the events.
- Plan an exchange with a class of a different age.

     One senior adult class provided rotating "huggers" in a preschool class. The hugger had no teaching responsibilities but gave children a grandparent figure. Another adult class adopted a children's class, praying for the teachers regularly and asking the children to visit their class and share something they learned. They also gave a party for the children's class. And another adult class met for four weeks with a senior high class, alternating teachers and classrooms. It enriched both classes!
- On a regular basis (perhaps early fall at "promotion" time) as a class, review what you have accomplished or learned during the year, preparing posters to be displayed in the hallway or a common area.
- Develop a study plan and publicize the dates and subjects. (See chapter 7.)
- Exchange rooms with another class in order to have a room appropriate to the size of your class.
- Select a guest teacher who will appeal to class members and contract for a specific teaching time. Select someone as liaison between teacher and class.
- On occasion a class may be healed by dividing, particularly when part of the class wants more in-depth study. To ease such decisions, plan for social times when members of both classes continue to meet together. Review chapter 4 for suggestions on dividing classes.

Acknowledging the completed life cycle

When a caterpillar comes to the close of its life cycle we celebrate. However, when a class completes a life cycle we often continue to force it to be a "caterpillar." Note the chart "Life

Cycle of a Class," at the end of chapter 3. Life cycle completion naturally occurs with older adult classes. It may also happen to younger classes that were formed around specific needs if those needs have been met or if the class no longer meets those needs.

Adult classes attract persons only a few years younger than the youngest charter members, and nearly all ongoing adult classes die within a few years following the death of the last charter member[1].

As the numbers dwindle, older classes may stop meeting each Sunday and meet monthly or quarterly with dinner and get-togethers. It is important to continue the supporting relationships that developed through the years. Encourage members to sit in on other classes during the Sunday school hour, but recognize that the new class will not take the place of those well-established relationships of the old class. Those relationships need to continue in an organized fashion.

Ailing younger classes that no longer have a focused purpose may need to readjust their focus or discontinue meeting. Work with other classes to see that remaining members become a part of a caring group that will meet their needs.

Although it is natural for a class to die, the process need not be painful. Help class members recognize the history of the class. Celebrate the accomplishments of the class with the whole congregation.

In order to remain healthy, your class needs to regularly review its current responsibilities as a class. What is your purpose as a class? Are you fulfilling that purpose? Do you need to redirect your purpose? Too often classes are like the roots of a tree once grown in a pot, reaching only inward and not extending beyond earlier constraints.

CHAPTER 11

Training Helps for Pastors and Church Leaders

Because adult classes often seem to carry on without any training, we usually ignore this important ministry. However, if we are to reach out to new adults and keep the ones we have, our classes must be vital communities of growing faith.

You may use this book in several ways as you prepare your adult class leaders and teachers. First, purchase a copy of this book for each class, asking each officer and teacher to read the first two chapters and other materials pertinent to their responsibility. Encourage officers and teachers to purchase their own copy so that it may be used for reference throughout their time of service in the class. You might even develop a self-study program for them to follow on their own. If you do this, plan an opportunity for those studying it at home to come together and share ideas they glean during their study.

Even more benefit will come from a group training where you use the book. In setting a time for such a training, recognize the limitations of time in the lives of today's adults. You will probably have the best attendance during the regular Sunday school hour. This is a time they normally reserve for church activities, and child care is available. In order to involve all of the officers and/or teachers, arrange for all classes to meet together in a large assembly room for a special program while you conduct the training elsewhere.

Training for class officers

1) Review adult categories at the end of chapter 3 and ask the officers to jot down persons in the church who fall into each of the categories.

2) Use materials in chapters 1, 2, and 3 for background information. Recommend that they read the chapters for more complete understanding.

3) Review the Leader/Officer Guidelines in chapter 5. If officers represent several classes, divide them into smaller groups according to their responsibilities and ask them to concentrate on their own areas. Officers responsible for program planning need to give special attention to chapter 7.

4) Divide the participants into two sub-groups. Ask one group to review chapter 8 and one to review chapter 9. Each sub-group will report back to the whole group.

5) Ask the officers from each class to meet together briefly to:
   —decide on a mutual meeting time to do some short-term and long-range planning for their class.
   —decide on *one* special thing they have learned during this training that they want to implement in their class. They will write this in a short sentence to use during the closing of the training.

6) Close the training with the following prayer, asking each class group of officers to speak aloud, at the appropriate time, the sentence they wrote about what they want to implement in their class.

Leader: We come to you, O God, with new vision. We recognize our calling as leaders of adults in this church, and we look to you for guidance. There are several ways that we believe we can strengthen our classes. We mention these now.

Class Officers: *Read the sentences each officer group wrote.*

Leader: Thank you for this opportunity to serve you. May we go out from here to guide the adults. Give us a new desire to learn as we guide. Amen.

Training for teachers

1) Ask the teachers to find one or two persons nearby to discuss the following questions:

- Recall an adult class that you attended that bored you. What happened in the class? What did the room look like? Did you have an opportunity to respond to what was presented? Do you even recall the subject and what was taught?
- What was something that you learned from a mistake you made?
- Think of at least three ways we learn every day without a teacher.
- Think of a time you taught something from a prepared lesson. What did you learn as you prepared the lesson?
- How have you changed your life because of what you have learned as you have prepared lessons?
- Does learning take place every time someone teaches? Who learns? Wrestle with the idea of learning versus teaching.

2) For foundational understanding, use materials from chapters 1 and 2. Use the beginning of chapter 6 for background information on adult learning.
3) Depending on the amount of time available, use material from chapter 3 appropriate to each class or assign it for reading.
4) Review "Forming good questions and answers" and "Teaching with discussion" in chapter 6.
5) Review the teacher tools in chapter 6 and experiment with several methods.
6) Review chapter 6 (Planning Resources) or assign it for reading, depending on the time available.
7) Close with a method of using prayer from pages 45-46.

Adult Class Information Survey

Date _____

Name(s) #1 _____

       #2 _____

Address _____

City/Zip _____ Phone _____

Birthday(s) #1 _____ #2 _____ Wedding Anniversary _____

Occupation #1_____ Phone _____

Occupation #2 _____ Phone _____

Special skills/hobbies #1 _____

Special skills/hobbies #2 _____

Past church/class leadership #1 _____

Past church/class leadership #2 _____

Other family members and ages _____

_____

_____

I (We) would like to see our class plan for:

These subjects for study: _____

    I am willing to ☐ collect information ☐ teach on _____

Mission projects: _____

    I will ☐ assist in planning ☐ help carry out such projects

Local church projects: _____

    I will ☐ assist in planning ☐ participate in these projects

Spiritual enrichment experiences: _____

    I will ☐ assist in planning ☐ participate in these experiences

Fellowship activities: _____

    I will ☐ assist in planning ☐ participate in these activities. I suggest this frequency
    and time for fellowship activities: _____

    _____

If asked to participate in leadership of our class, I have an interest in these positions:

Person # 1 _____

Person # 2 _____

Adult Study Interest Survey

I prefer that the majority of the classes be   but I'd also enjoy some

- ☐   DISCUSSION   ☐
- ☐   LECTURE   ☐
- ☐   PANEL   ☐
- ☐   EXPERIENTIAL ACTIVITIES   ☐

I like to study primarily   but I'd enjoy a little

- ☐   BIBLE   ☐
- ☐   CURRENT ISSUES   ☐
- ☐   SOCIAL CONCERNS   ☐
- ☐   ENVIRONMENTAL CONCERNS   ☐
- ☐   RELATIONSHIPS   ☐
- ☐   FAMILY RELATIONS   ☐
- ☐   PRAYER/SPIRITUAL GROWTH   ☐
- ☐   (other) _____   ☐

Some specific subjects I really have an interest in are _____

_____

I ☐ do ☐ do not like to have student preparation ahead of class.

I prefer to study one subject for ☐ one week ☐ two weeks ☐ a month ☐ a quarter

I like to have ☐ a regular teacher ☐ several teachers that rotate ☐ class members teaching ☐ persons outside class ☐ church staff as teachers ☐ _____.

I enjoy having our class schedule arranged in the following manner (list order by number and leave off those you do not think necessary for our class):

- _____ Refreshments
- _____ Announcements
- _____ Prayer and prayer concerns

- _____ Devotions
- _____ Study time
- _____ Singing

Additional suggestions for our class: _____

_____

_____

Name (optional) _____

Study Plan

Class _____ Date/Time Frame _____

Teacher(s) _____

Teachers not using regular curriculum for classes are asked to fill out this Study Plan and submit it to the Education Office. This gives the Education Committee an opportunity to review the plan and assist the teachers in resourcing. It can also be used by the Education Office when prospective class members or others question the content of the class.

Subject:

Resources:

Learning Activities:

Additional Comments:

Adult Class Study Outline

CLASS: _____

SUNDAY	THEME	LEADER

 **Adult Self-Directed Study**

FORM FOR PLANNING

Use the suggestions below to gather information for a self-directed study program. You may want to plan a specific time for persons working on self-directed study programs to come together to share with each other. Be sure to plan recognition when a course is finished.

Study Name _____

- Scripture background on subject _____

_____

- Denominational and local church information on subject _____

_____

- Resources (books, videos, magazine articles) and questions for comprehension. If you want to copy articles or sections of a book, write or call publisher for permission.

Resource #1 _____

Questions: _____

_____

Resource #2 _____

Questions: _____

_____

Resource #3 _____

Questions: _____

_____

Field trip or hands-on experience you might require for course: ___

_____

Follow-up information you will require: _____

_____

_____

Expected time for completion of study _____

Times for personal review of study progress _____

Time(s) for persons in study to meet for interaction _____

Time for recognition of completion _____

Might this subject be one you would ask the person to teach a class on? _____

List additional requirements and plans on back.

Lesson Plan

Subject _____ Date _____

Special needs of class members that this session will meet _____
_____

Scripture _____

Reflections on scripture and how it applies to learners _____
_____
_____

Main idea or thought I wish to get across _____
_____

Other ideas/thoughts stemming from main idea _____
_____
_____
_____

How can the learners experience the main idea? (Use action words) _____
_____
_____

Materials we will need _____
_____

Special room arrangements _____
Additional contacts and preparation _____
_____

Basic presentation of content using back of page or additional pages.

— —

HOW DID IT GO? (Fill in after class.)

Positive things _____
_____

Trouble spots _____
_____

Evidence of growth _____
_____

Meeting Action Sheet

Name of group: _____

Objectives: _____

AGENDA	PERSONS IN ATTENDANCE

DECISIONS REACHED

FUTURE ACTION REQUIRED	PERSON RESPONSIBLE	COMPLETION DATE

Plan-For-Action

Project Name _____ Date of Event _____

Description _____

_____

_____

Purpose/goal(s) _____

_____

_____

To accomplish	Deadline
☐ _____	_____
☐ _____	_____
☐ _____	_____
☐ _____	_____
☐ _____	_____
☐ _____	_____
☐ _____	_____
☐ _____	_____
☐ _____	_____

Person(s) involved	Phone	Responsibility
_____	_____	_____
_____	_____	_____
_____	_____	_____
_____	_____	_____
_____	_____	_____
_____	_____	_____

Evaluation/future suggestions _____

_____

_____

Retreat Pre-Planning

General purpose of a retreat: A retreat is specific time spent with persons pursuing a common interest, in a place apart from the ordinary events of life. A Christian retreat includes experiences that bring a new awareness of the presence of God.

Who will be involved? _____

What do we hope will happen? _____

_____

Planning Committee members   Phone

_____   _____

_____   _____

_____   _____

_____   _____

Content possibilities: Curriculum _____

_____

    Resource person(s) _____ Phone _____

    _____ Phone _____

    Group building activities _____

    _____

    _____

    Other activities (include music) _____

    _____

    _____

    _____

Amount of time ☐ one day ☐ overnight ☐ weekend ☐ Other_____

Transportation _____

_____

Child care plans _____

Date preference _____ Alternative dates _____

Publicity Plan_____

_____

_____

_____

Meals: ☐ cook in ☐ catered ☐ eat out ☐ each provide own

Food possibilities _____

_____

_____

Possible schedule—include worship, study, play and/or free time:

_____   _____

_____   _____

_____   _____

_____   _____

_____   _____

_____   _____

_____   _____

_____   _____

_____   _____

Some possible retreat rules: _____

_____

_____

Facility requirements ☐ cabin/bunks ☐ private rooms ☐ meeting room (size _____)

    ☐ dining with others ☐ dining in private group ☐ chapel ☐ outdoor facility

    requirements _____ ☐ child care facility

    _____ ☐ other _____

Facility possibilities _____

_____

Budget:

Some ways to follow up/evaluate: _____

_____

Work Camp/Mission Project Pre-Planning

Goals we hope will be accomplished with this event:

For participants: _____

_____

For recipients: _____

_____

Who will be involved? _____

Planning Committee members   Phone

_____   _____

_____   _____

_____   _____

_____   _____

What sort of experience is the group capable of? (heavy/light physical work, VBS leadership, construction, medical/dental, etc.) _____

_____

What ages will be involved in the actual work? (Will teenagers or children of families be involved?) _____

Will we need child care? _____ Whom will we get for this? _____

Where will child care be held? _____

Length of time for event? _____

Date possibilities _____

Where (with what agencies) might this take place? _____

_____

Transportation _____

_____

Prior to event:

Group-building activities _____

_____

Training activities _____

_____

Dedication of mission (in worship, just before leaving, etc.) _____

_____

_____

In-church publicity _____

_____

Community publicity before/after (Remember that publicity about your mission spreads Christ and your church's mission to the community.) _____

_____

Some possible event rules. _____

_____

_____

Additional plans to be made (If you will coordinate your own work, consider supplies, equipment, schedules, lodging, food, spiritual enrichment, etc.):

Budget:

Some ways to follow up/evaluate _____

_____

Getting into the Bible

We can use the Bible as a tool in our faith journey if we spend time becoming familiar with its content and the way that it is set up. The following exercise will help you to find the sections of the Bible. As you learn which books are in which section, you will be able to locate passages with ease.

Getting Started

Turn to the table of contents in your Bible. The Bible is made up of various sections or books. It is like a mini-library, all bound together in one volume. In fact, the word *Bible* means *books*. If at any time you have difficulty in finding a passage quickly, feel free to turn to the table of contents. You might want to place a marker there so that you can find it easily.

The way that a Bible reference is written helps us to locate it. For example, when we write John 3:16, we know that the reference is in the book of John, in the third chapter and the sixteenth verse. If we are concentrating on only part of a verse, then we may use "a" or "b" after the verse number, such as Matthew 10:5*b*. When the reference is for more than one verse (Luke 2:1-20), we write it with a hyphen, indicating that we are looking for verses one through twenty. If we want selected verses in the same chapter that do not follow one another, we use commas between them (Psalm 8:1, 3). If the passage continues into the next chapter, we use the word *through* (Matthew 1:18 through 2:12). If we are looking for sections of verses in the same book, but in different chapters, we use a semicolon, such as these stories of Jesus' healing ministry: Luke 17:11-19; 18:35-43.

Old and New Testaments

The books of the Bible are divided into two sections, the Old Testament, which was written before Jesus' birth (in the front of the Bible) and the New Testament, which was written after Jesus' death (in the back of the Bible).

Using the table of contents, locate the beginning of the New Testament and then turn to it. Mark this place with your finger and close the book. Look at the edge of the Bible and discover that there are more pages in the Old Testament than in the New Testament. The Old Testament covers many more years than the New Testament.

Books of Wisdom

Take your finger out of the Bible and reopen the book to the middle. You will probably find the Psalms. This book is found in the center of the Bible and is generally referred to as wisdom literature. The wisdom books include Job through Solomon (or the Song of Songs).

Creation and Law

With the Bible still opened to the middle, divide the front half in half again. You will probably find yourself near the end of the book of Deuteronomy. The books in your left hand will include the books that tell us about creation and the law that the Jewish people of Jesus' day lived by. These books also include the stories of people who lived long ago, before Israel became a nation.

Old Testament History

The books in your right hand will include books of the Old Testament history (Joshua through Esther). These come between the books of creation and law and the wisdom books. They tell of the rulers of Israel and the trials and problems that they had as they fought with other nations and among themselves.

Prophets

The remaining books in the Old Testament (following the wisdom books) are books of the prophets (Isaiah through Malachi). Prophets are persons who spoke to the people for God, and there were many of these during Old Testament times. They are divided into what we call the major and minor prophets. They are called this not because of their importance, but because of the size of each book. The major prophets are larger books and are in the front; the minor prophets have fewer pages and are the last books of the Old Testament.

New Testament History (Gospel and Acts)

Close the Bible now and open it again in the center. Divide the back half in half again (the pages in your right hand). You will find that you are near the beginning of the New Testament (Matthew).

Holding only the pages of the New Testament, divide this section in half. The New Testament also has two parts. The pages in your left hand can be called the history part of the New Testament. This includes the four gospels which tell us about Jesus' life and teachings (Matthew, Mark, Luke, and John). We call these the Gospels (or good news) because they tell of the good news of Jesus' coming. The first half of the New Testament also includes Acts, which is a book that tells about the early church after Jesus died.

The Letters

The remaining part of the New Testament (the pages in your right hand) is primarily made up of letters written to the people of some of the first churches. Some of these letters have the names of the people to whom they are written as the titles; other have the names of the persons whom we believe to have been the writers.

Revelation

Turn to the last book in the Bible, Revelation. It is the only apocalyptic book in the New Testament. This is a type of writing that was popular in the last centuries before Christ, when everyone was discouraged and waiting for the messiah. Daniel is an apocalyptic book in the Old Testament, but most of the apocalyptic books of that time were not included in the Bible.

Revelation was written during a time when the Christians who refused to worship the Roman emperor were placed in prisons and killed. Apocalyptic writing uses a lot of symbols and imagery. People today have many different views about the meanings of the symbols in this book. Although the true meanings of the author may be lost, we do know that he was trying to tell the people that although things may have seemed very bad for them, God would win out in the end.

—FROM *HOW TO TRAIN VOLUNTEER TEACHERS* BY DELIA HALVERSON.
COPYRIGHT © 1991 BY ABINGDON PRESS. USED BY PERMISSION.

Guidelines for Ongoing Support Groups

Support groups are effective ways to develop and grow in our Christian faith. Support groups may evolve out of a study group, be organized around a special need or life situation, or come together with a common cause. Some groups center on developing their prayer life, some on study, and some help each other live out Christianity in their everyday world by being accountable to each other. Christ gave us the prime example of a support group when he selected his disciples. Although the disciples came from many walks of life and their personalities were varied, their common cause was Christ's cause.

Unlike Christ's group of disciples, however, small support groups today should not be centered around a particular leader but should develop a common group leadership. This does not mean that every person in the group must lead, but that everyone's importance is felt equally and that the leadership is shared by as many of the group members who feel that they would like to try.

How often to meet?

This can be determined by the group. Most groups meet weekly or twice a month. In order to develop a close relationship in the group, you will want to meet at least twice a month. This is particularly true if you follow a continuous plan of study. Monthly meetings may work if each session of study is independent of the others. Groups are usually more effective in the home. Some groups select to meet at one home for a month and then change, and other groups change with each meeting.

Who leads the group?

An appointed coordinator can help the group to run smoother. This person becomes the liaison between the group and the education committee. However, this leadership should be passed around at least annually. This keeps the group from becoming known as "John Doe's Group." Through this coordinator, the education committee can give support and resources to the group, and the group has some sort of accountability.

Session leadership may be passed among the members, or one person may take the leadership for a given amount of time.

What to study?

Take inventory of interests and needs within the group and check your local church library and denominational source for books or curriculum on the subject you choose to study.

What format should you follow?

Each group becomes individual in format. The format should include some sort of study, sharing time, and prayer time. This helps the members to support one another.

What size?

Jesus chose twelve disciples. An advantage to multiples of four is that you may divide into fours at times of discussion. In fours, the quiet person feels free to talk, and the talkative person usually does not dominate the conversation. However, if your group is smaller than eight, you may want to plan discussion time as one group. When the group gets much larger than twelve, some persons may feel reluctant to speak out, afraid that there will not be time for everyone. When support groups get too large, they sometimes divide, still getting together for some social activity.

How can you give importance to the group?

Make the group one of your priorities. Set the time aside for group meetings and allow only emergencies to keep you from attending.

Support will develop, and the group members should begin to feel that they can call on one another in time of need, even in the middle of the night.

Confidentiality is of prime importance. Nothing said in a support group should be repeated outside the group.

Be sure that everyone participates and no one dominates. Feel free to remind each other of this in a loving way when one person continually dominates the conversations. Everyone has a right to his or her own opinion, and we must respect that right. Encourage and respect "dumb questions."

What is the life expectation of a group?

Some small groups last over many years, and some only a year or so. There is nothing that says a group should last any specific time. Sometimes the persons within the group move in different directions and a group may need to dissolve. Members of the group should also feel free to leave if their circumstances make this necessary. Committing yourself to such a group does not indicate that you expect to remain together forever, but it is important to make the group a priority while you remain a part of the group.

Steps to organizing a small group of adults

1. or 2. Decide the type of group and the purpose: study, service, support, or spiritual.
2. or 1. Consider the persons who might be a part of this group. Examine their needs. Invite persons to participate.
3. Plan the first meeting. Include a get-acquainted time and a discussion of what members would like in the group as well as worship and study experiences desired.
4. In the next meeting or two, develop a group covenant. This covement will state the expectations of the group and the steps that each member is willing to take to fulfill those expectations.

The covenant might include:
the purpose of this group;
how this group is related to the whole church family;
the degree of confidentiality within the group;
who can join and when;
the time of meetings, including opening and closing times;
the form and content of the meetings (support, tasks, study, prayer, service, and so forth);
an outline of details (such as the availability of childcare, refreshments, and so forth);
who will lead and realistic expectations of leaders;
the amount of preparation expected of members and leaders prior to the meeting time;
the frequency with which this covenant will need review.

—FROM *LEADER IN THE CHURCH SCHOOL TODAY,* VOL. 4, NO. 2 (FALL 1991), 28,
BY DELIA HALVERSON. COPYRIGHT © 1991 BY GRADED PRESS. USED BY PERMISSION.

A Teacher's Prayer Calendar

Thank God for all your students
and allow your love for them
to EXPLODE!

Sunday	Monday	Tuesday	Wednesday	Thursday	Friday	Saturday
Praise God!	Pray For:	Pray For:	Pray For:	Pray For:	Pray For:	Pray For:

Your church and your teaching ministry,
and allow God to work through you.
Share God's grace.

Adapted from *Teaching Prayer in the Classroom* by Delia Halverson. Copyright © 1989 Abingdon Press.
How to Train Volunteer Teachers, copyright © 1991 by Abingdon Press.

NOTES

1. Educating Adults—More Than Book Learning

1. Eugene C. Roehlkepartain, *The Teaching Church* (Nashville: Abingdon Press, 1993), 130.
2. Peter L. Benson and Carolyn H. Eklin, *Effective Christian Education: A National Study of Congregations* (Minneapolis: Search Institute, 1990).
3. Ibid., 54.

2. Exploring Faith Development

1. James W. Fowler, *Stages of Faith: The Psychology of Human Development and the Quest for Meaning* (New York: Harper & Row, 1981), chapters 15–21.
2. Delia T. Halverson, *Helping Your Teen Develop Faith* (Valley Forge: Judson, 1985), 27-29.
3. Eugene C. Roehlkepartain and Dorothy Williams, *Exploring Faith Maturity* (Minneapolis: Search Institute, 1990), 5.
4. Eugene C. Roehlkepartain, *The Teaching Church* (Nashville: Abingdon Press, 1993), 36-37.

3. Characterizing Adult Sunday School Classes

1. Warren J. Hartman, *Five Audiences: Identifying Groups in Your Church* (Nashville: Abingdon Press, 1987).
2. Eugene C. Roehlkepartain, *The Teaching Church* (Nashville: Abingdon Press, 1993), 79.
3. Dick Murray, *Strengthening the Adult Sunday School Class.* Copyright © by Abingdon Press, 1981, p. 32-33. Used by Permission.

4. Forming New Adult Classes

1. Cheryl Reames, "Adults: Reach Them, Keep Them," Nashville: Graded Press, 1986. (leaflet from Cokesbury)

5. Guiding Leaders and Officers

1. Jack Seymour, Margaret Ann Crain and Joseph V. Crockett, *Educating Christians* (Nashville: Abingdon Press, 1993), 170.

6. Teaching Tools

1. Jack Seymour, Margaret Ann Crain and Joseph V. Crockett, *Educating Christians* (Nashville: Abingdon Press, 1993), 142-44.
2. Dick Murray, *Strengthening the Adult Sunday School Class* (Nashville: Abingdon Press, 1981), 94.
3. From Delia Halverson, "Teach Me How to Pray," *Youth!* February, 1990, Graded Press.

7. Planning Resources

1. Charles R. Foster in *The Ministry of the Volunteer Teacher* (Nashville: Abingdon Press, 1986), 70; and modified and expanded by Josephine M. Biggerstaff in "How to Choose a Study," *Teacher in the Church Today* Sept. 1992.

10. Healing Sick Classes

1. Dick Murray, *Strengthening the Adult Sunday School Class* (Nashville: Abingdon Press, 1981), 30.

BIBLIOGRAPHY

Benson, Peter L. and Carolyn H. Eklin. Effective Christian Education: A National Study of Protestant Congregations—Summary Report on Faith, Loyalty, and Congregational Life. Minneapolis: Search Institute, 1990. (See Roehlkepartain Exploring Christian Education Effectiveness, below.)

Foster, Charles R. *The Ministry of the Volunteer Teacher*. Nashville: Abingdon Press, 1986.

Fowler, James W. *Stages of Faith: The Psychology of Human Development and the Quest for Meaning*. New York: Harper & Row, 1981.

Halverson, Delia. *Helping Your Teen Develop Faith*. Valley Forge: Judson, 1985.

Halverson, Delia. *How to Train Volunteer Teachers*. Nashville: Abingdon Press, 1991.

Halverson, Delia. *Leader in the Church School Today,* vol. 4, no. 2 (Fall 1991).

Halverson, Delia. *Teaching Prayer in the Classroom*. Nashville: Abingdon Press, 1989.

Harman, Shirly. *Retreat Planning Made Easy: A Resource for Christian Retreats*. Minneapolis: Augsburg, 1991.

Hartman, Warren J. *Five Audiences*. Nashville: Abingdon Press, 1987.

Leypoldt, Martha. *40 Ways to Teach in Groups*. Valley Forge: Judson Press, 1967.

Murray, Dick. *Strengthening the Adult Sunday School Class*. Nashville: Abingdon Press, 1981.

———. *Teaching the Bible to Adults and Youth*. Nashville: Abingdon Press, 1987.

Osmer, Richard. *Teaching for Faith*. Louisville, Ky.: Westminster/John Knox Press, 1991.

Owens, Joanne. *The Official Sunday School Teachers Handbook*. Colorado Springs: Meriwether Publishing, 1988.

Reames, Cheryl. "Adults: Reach Them, Keep Them." Nashville: Graded Press, 1986.

Reichter, Arlo. *The Group Retreat Book*. Loveland, Co.: Group Publishers, 1983.

Roehlkepartain, Eugene C. *Exploring Christian Education Effectiveness*. Minneapolis: Search Institute, 1990. (Workbook for assessing Christian education program in local church plus workshop outline.)

———. *The Teaching Church*. Nashville: Abingdon Press, 1993.

Schultz, Thom & Joani. *Why Nobody Learns Much of Anything at Church: And How to Fix It*. Loveland: Group Publishers, 1993.

Seymour, Jack, Margaret Ann Crain and Joseph V. Crockett. *Educating Christians*. Nashville: Abingdon Press, 1993.

Shawchuck, Norman, Reuben Job, and Robert Doherty. *How to Conduct a Spiritual Life Retreat*. Nashville: Discipleship Resources, 1986.

Vogel, Linda. *Teaching Older Adults*. Nashville: Discipleship Resources, 1989.

Westerhoff, John. *Will Our Children Have Faith*. HarperSan Francisco, 1983.

Williams, Melvin. *Where Faith Seeks Understanding*. Nashville: Abingdon Press, 1987.

Additional Resources

Bible Teacher Kit (maps, resource pages, videocassette). Nashville: Cokesbury, 1994.

Profiles of Congregational Life. Minneapolis: Search Institute, 1-800-888-7828 (in-depth survey service for local congregations on issues of faith maturity, congregational effectiveness, and Christian education.)